What Helped Me When My Loved One Died

What Helped Me When My Loved One Died

Earl A. Grollman

BEACON PRESS 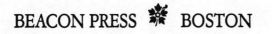 BOSTON

Beacon Press books are published under the auspices
of the Unitarian Universalist Association, 25 Beacon
Street, Boston, Massachusetts 02108

Published simultaneously in Canada by
Fitzhenry & Whiteside Limited, Toronto

Printed in the United States of America

(paperback) 9 8 7 6 5 4 3 2

Library of Congress Cataloging in Publication Data

Main entry under title.

What helped me when my loved one died.

    1. Consolation—Addresses, essays, lectures.
2. Grief—Addresses, essays, lectures. I. Grollman, Earl A., comp.
BV4905.2.W48   248.8'6   80-68166
ISBN 0-8070-3229-8   AACR2

Dedicated to the memories of

Alexander
Bea
Bella
Cara
David
Diana
Edgar
George
Gerson
Glen
Jimmy
Joseph
Kathleen
Lawrence
Mark
Michelle
Samuel
Seppli
Sheila

Words of Encouragement

In this sad world of ours, sorrow comes to all . . .
It comes with bitterest agony . . .
Perfect relief is not possible, except with time.
You cannot now realize that you will ever feel better . . .
And yet this is a mistake.
You are sure to be happy again,
To know this, which is certainly true,
Will make you come less miserable now.
I have experienced enough to know what I say.
                              Abraham Lincoln

Three of Abraham Lincoln's sons died: Edward, age 4; William, age 11; and Thomas, age 18.

Contents

FOREWORD

BY EARL A. GROLLMAN

Recently I addressed a group of widows and widowers in the Pacific Northwest. I had finished my talk and responded to their many questions on grief and bereavement when the chairman hurried over to me. "Our next speaker has not arrived. Could you please cover for her? I'm sure that she will be here shortly."

I told the audience, "I've talked enough. You have already heard *me*. Let me hear from *you*. You're the real experts in the area of dying and death. Tell me — what helped *you* when your loved one died?"

What a beautiful sharing experience! Stories unfolded revealing the impact of loneliness and alienation, and of finding a small ray of light in the darkness of their lives. Heads began to nod. The others had had similar experiences. As they shared, these many solitary people spoke with one voice. It was a spiritual experience — unmatched in any church or synagogue.

The focus had shifted from death to survival and a developing desire to *stay* alive. Someone characterized our session as "Lemonade from Lemons" — and it was that, bittersweet but surprisingly refreshing.

Thanatologists who study the science of death have been effective in defining the stages of grief. But as the contributors to this book (many of them experts in the field of death and dying) said, "No one ever asked: What helped *me* when my loved one died." As you read of their adjustments to the loss of separation, you may better understand how you might rescue yourself from drowning in the sea of private sorrow.

You probably never thought that you would be adrift in life's most difficult situation. The idea of a loved one dying is too terrifying to contemplate. Now you are utterly lost — emotionally unprepared. You need many things; not the least is the knowledge that you are not alone in your feelings. You need to know that there is help available. That's what these chapters are all about.

This is not a "how to" book. No one can tell someone else how to grieve. There is no "normal" time span over which healing takes place. Grief is a process. The contributors to this volume have varied backgrounds and life experiences. However, in their diverse descriptions of bereavement there is one unifying theme — coping wisely with the pain of separation.

No one can keep you from suffering; but you do not have to suffer for the wrong reasons. Our hope is that you will choose what to remember of the past, cherish the joys of the present, and plan a future to which you can look forward.

TEN HELPFUL GUIDELINES

These guidelines are a cooperative effort by the editor and the many contributors to this book. The contributor's words are in quotation marks. It is our hope that these guidelines will help you in your growing process as you move from helplessness to hopefulness.

1. *Accept Your Emotions*

Death hurts. It's so difficult to say goodbye — to realize that in your lifetime you will never see or touch your loved one again. Why pretend that you are not experiencing terrible inner turmoil? Your emotions are a natural response to the death of a loved one.

Reactions to death are varied and contradictory, appearing in widely contrasting combinations. Many feelings may be expressed in the space of a few moments. "My emotions went on a roller coaster. One minute I would be weeping, the next minute I would feel almost normal."

The way you confront the death of your loved one will depend on many factors: how recent the death, the quality of the relationship, the manner in which you normally handle stress, and the support of your family and friends. That's why "the only script is no script. Everyone copes in his or her own way. There is no prescribed way to mourn. General stages, perhaps. But within these phases, there is tremendous variability."

Initially you may be in shock. Not only has your loved one died, you feel dead, too. You are literally stunned, as if under anesthesia. "I felt like a spectator in a drama. I had to keep reminding myself that all this fuss was about my wife. She was dead. I just couldn't understand what was happening around me. I felt paralyzed."

Guilt feelings are perhaps the most demanding, erratic, and the hardest to cope with reactions to death. "Because I hadn't been able to sustain my baby's life, I felt a public flogging would have been appropriate."

"I didn't do enough for my husband."

"I feel relieved that her terrible pain is over and I no longer have to take care of her and she now is at peace. And yet, I feel guilty for feeling this way . . ."

"If only I had called the doctor sooner . . ."

These feelings of guilt are common but they will not bring your loved one back to life. The past is over. You don't change circumstances by replaying the ninth inning over and over. Remember that everyone errs now and then. To forgive (even yourself) is divine.

Emotional stress affects your physical well-being. Headaches, intestinal upsets, dizzy spells, and insomnia may be your body's response to the death of your loved one. The pain is real. At this crucial stage of your life, you should have your family physician check you over from time to time.

You may experience many variations on the theme of pain. If you are capable of affection, you will suffer from the separation. Grief is the other side of the coin of life. Accepting such emotions as natural is the beginning of healthful mourning. "I questioned my sanity until I understood that these feelings are normal."

There also may be moments of denial. "It's a nightmare. When I wake up, I'll find that it really didn't happen." It may be your way of saying, "I don't want to face it. Not now, anyway."

Panic may set in. You are overburdened. You just want to run away — anywhere. Maybe, take your own life. "What will I do, how will I stand it?" You agonize over simple decisions, things that you used to do with ease. A woman said to her doctor: "'I don't know if I can get through this day; how will I ever survive the rest of my life?' He looked at me and, instead of saying something dumb, treated me like a friend and said, 'This must be the most terrible thing in the world.' His words, spoken as a friend, were comforting because they meant he was trying to understand."

Resentment is a temporary emotional state caused by frustration, a natural part of the grief process. Anger and sadness are very closely related. You should not feel guilty when you feel or express "rage" or "fury."

You may find yourself becoming angry with everyone around you. At the doctor and nurses: "A well-meaning new resident... told us [our daughter] was doing fine and we would have her home soon. Anyone with eyes ... knew she was dying."

Or at God: "At times like this everyone questions the will of God. Why did God let this happen?"

At your friends: "I haven't seen them since the funeral."

You may even want to lash out at the person who died. "It's so easy for him. Buried so comfortably in the cemetery. Leaving me with all these problems and responsibilities."

You could be angry with yourself. "Other people seem to manage so well. What's wrong with me?"

2. *Express Your Feelings*

It is not enough to recognize your conflicting emotions; you must deal with them openly. A feeling that is denied expression is not destroyed; it remains with you and often erupts at inappropriate times. To intellectualize your reactions and by-pass your emotional stress is to prolong the agony and delay the grief process. Acknowledging pain when you feel it is much better for your long-term emotional health.

Be honest about your feelings. "I couldn't say the words *dead* or *widow*. I couldn't admit that my life had changed so abruptly. Now I have to accept the fact that my husband will never come back. And it hurts."

It does hurt to use words like *die* and *dead*, but euphemisms like *expire, pass away, pass on,* and *depart* may be evasions that indicate an inability to deal honestly with the situation. But you must confront reality. Your loved one is *dead.*

Put your feelings into words. "My big mistake was bottling up my reactions. When people asked me how I was doing, I would say 'fine' even though I couldn't think of a single reason to go on living. Feelings festered inside me until I could scream them out loud. I felt better then."

Putting your thoughts on paper can be therapeutic.

"Writing down our experience has helped us to do some further grief work together."

"Reading and rereading the diary has been such an effective grieving tool for me."

"My journal is my special friend, my instrument for survival."

You have a right to cry if you want to. It is a natural expression of grief for men as well as women and children. Weeping helps to express the depth of despair that follows the slow realization that the death of your beloved is not just a bad dream. Don't take pride in stoicism or excellent self-control. Crying is the emptying out of the emotions. "The healing began when a friend embraced me, leaving some of his tears upon my cheek."

Everyone needs outlets to discharge pent-up feelings. Don't count on tranquilizers to do the grief work for you. If you need any sedation, get a prescription for a small amount of tranquilizers and stay in touch with your doctor. Alcohol, too, only delays the mourning process. There are no detours around the pain of separation.

3. *Don't Expect Miracles Overnight*

Allow sufficient time for the grieving period to run its course. The process is never the same for any two people.

Don't compare yourself with others in similar positions. Their smiles may not reveal the depth of their sorrow.

Heal in your own way and in your own time. Insist that others give you this freedom as well. Be yourself. You don't need to pretend grief beyond the time you need to grieve. Nor do you need feign recovery before you are recovered.

"I made a valuable *new* friend — time. The sadness can seem interminable, the pain relentless, but it does pass. The tears still come, unexpectedly, but with less intensity and less frequency. At first the sudden waves of sadness knocked me down, but I have learned to stand up to them — all because of time."

4. *If You Have Children, Bring Them into the Grieving Process*

They should not be shielded from tragedy. Death is a crisis that should be shared by all members of the family. Children too often are forgotten by grieving adults. Silence and secrecy deprive them of an important opportunity to share grief. When in your heartache you overlook your children's feelings, you heighten their sense of isolation. The youngsters need your help to sort out their emotions. When you discuss death with your children openly, you enable them to face reality without psychological defenses.

When a loved one dies, children often suffer the death of two people: the one who died and the parent or parents who are too absorbed in their own grief to notice their youngsters' needs. Let them know the reason for your tears and unhappiness. "Until my mother told me how terrible she felt about Daddy's death, I thought she was mad at me."

To mourn without fear or embarrassment can help both children and parents to accept the naturalness of the pangs of death. "In some ways it felt good to have Nicky so openly angry with me. He was expressing a lot of my guilty feelings."

Stories and fairy tales are not satisfactory explanations for the mystery of death. Never cover up with a fictitious or confusing interpretation that you will someday have to repudiate. For example, to say "Your father has gone away on a long journey" is to give the impression that he may someday return. "God took your young mother because the Lord needs good people with Him" will only encourage a deep resentment against a God who capriciously robbed children of a needed mother. Unhealthy explanations can create fear, doubt, and guilt, encouraging flights of fancy that are far more bizarre than reality. There is no greater need children have at this time than trust and truth.

There is no "right" and "proper" way to explain death to children. What is said is significant, but how it is said will have a greater bearing on whether your youngsters develop unnecessary fears or are able to accept, within their ability, the reality of death. Approach your child gently and with love. The tone of your voice — sympathetic, and kind — will communicate feelings more completely than any specific words.

Your children's most important source of security is *you*. Stay close to them, hug them, let them feel the warmth of your body. When words fail, the reaching out physically is the clearest communication of reassurance and comfort.

5. *Escaping into Loneliness Is the Wrong Solution*

If you stay alone too much, your home will become a protective shell that keeps you from facing the new challenges of life. Admittedly, the road ahead is unfamiliar. But you *must* leave your house. You might start with routine chores, like shopping, which do not demand too much exertion and concentration. "I didn't want to leave the apartment and meet people. It was too painful to hear how sorry they were about my child's death. Some even asked how she was — didn't know she died. But I made the leap. I couldn't hide anymore."

At the same time, don't overload the circuits. Look over your priorities. What are the things that have to be done now? Are your plans realistic? Don't punish yourself with unworkable and impractical tasks. Stick to what is important and necessary now. You need not worry too much about what is down the road. Take one step at a time outside your home. How about reconsidering that dinner invitation to your friend's home?

6. *Friends Are Important*

The common denominator of grief is loneliness. A special person — your loved one — can no longer share your life. You are bereft, alone.

Talk to a friend. Share your feelings. Let the right people know that you need support and feedback. They cannot bring you comfort unless you allow them to enter your sorrow.

"I will never cease to be amazed at how people found out about the death and what their reactions are; people that I hardly ever knew that have been writing and calling. I have found that people are sincerely interested in how I am doing; it's not just verbiage . . ."

"I was surprised that people had done very thoughtful things — neighborly outpouring of sympathy; our home was full of food, flowers, phone calls and visitors . . ."

"In the midst of my adversity, I noticed a tendency not

to bother anyone else with my misfortune. What a mistake. The love and support of family and friends in letters, phone calls, visits, and invitations were so gratifying and so enriching as to defy description. Reach out! Martyrdom is not a necessary part of the grief process . . ."

"[A friend's] presence and friendship . . . got me out of the black awful pit of grief and out where the sunshine could find me."

Holidays, birthdays, and anniversaries are especially difficult times to be alone. Plan ahead to spend these days with caring and understanding friends.

7. Help Yourself and Others Through Support Groups

At some point you may be disappointed in the reactions of your acquaintances, maybe even your close friends. You just don't hear from them so often anymore. They seem awkward and uneasy in your presence. Death is probably frightening to them. They may avoid your company. Just as you must forget about being your "old self," so you must now learn to accept people's differing reactions to death and realize that not everyone will meet your expectations.

That's why self-help groups have been successful in providing necessary emotional intervention through the crisis of death. People in these groups understand your fears and frustrations; they have been there before. Allow them to help you out of your isolation with a meaningful support network. Often, these sufferers become closer to you than your own family and friends. They share with you the time of your grief and help you to walk on your sorrowing path. You are no longer alone.

"It's hard to talk to other people. They change the subject. But in our support group we can talk to each other. A few tears are shed. They help and understand . . ."

"What carried us through? Families of Candlelighters. During her illness and after her death, I was the cause of numerous sore ears from long telephone conversations . . ."

"The Sudden Infant Death Syndrome meetings opened some very frail scars, reaffirming that grieving does not end. [The discussions at the meetings] emphasized that I am not the only human being on record that has experienced this kind of death . . . showed me that those who have lost loved ones can reach out to others and to me. I see that I am normal in what I am experiencing."

As you are being helped through your grief, you are beginning to share your strength, faith, hope, and experiences with others who are also struggling with loss, helping them.

"Interviewing other women who had stillbirths, hearing similarities to my own feelings, and feeling that I was helping them, helped me . . ."

"Her death gave me a new purpose — to form support networks to help during good times, uncertain times, and bad. To put my energies behind the efforts to find cures and controls for cancer, and improve the information available to other families . . ."

"What a neat way to celebrate my child's birthday, by sharing that day with others . . ."

"I must live for the future. There must be something I can do to help others."

8. *Counseling May Be Beneficial*

Sorrow leaves an imprint on the healthiest of personalities. You may need more than the warmth of a close friend or understanding of a fellow sufferer. A professional

11

counselor who is not emotionally attached to you may be more effective to assist you in viewing your problems in a clear perspective.

There is nothing wrong in obtaining help from a psychologist, psychiatrist, member of the clergy, mental health clinic, or social service organization. There is everything wrong with suffering needless pain when assistance may be available. Getting professional advice is not an admission of weakness but a demonstration of determination to help yourself during this critical period.

"I began weekly psychotherapy. I would recommend it to anyone in a similar situation . . ."

"Through counseling, we were able to recycle our feelings of guilt, of anger, and depression. We were able to see how we were changing with each visit."

9. *You Have to Be Nice to Yourself*

You need people. You also need moments of solitude to find yourself. Why not walk in a quiet place, paint a picture, read a book, or take a long, leisurely bath. "Silence is eloquent. Words can get in the way and be misunderstood. The best of life is the silence that needs no words." A little withdrawal and reflection allow you to return to your painful world more relaxed than you were before.

"It took awhile to realize that I needed to do what I felt was right at the time . . . that staying in bed one morning was not necessarily an escape."

Your faith may also help you to face and survive the inevitable moments of despair. For many, religion offers a philosophical base in the lonely encounter with helplessness and hopelessness. It affords a journey into the unknown, a spiritual glimpse into the world-to-be. Though reason cannot tell you why death occurs, and comforting words cannot wipe away your tears, faith offers consolation in death by giving honor to the deceased and guiding the bereaved in the reaffirmation of life:

"Talking with the minister helped me cut through my denial that nothing happened. He read the Twenty-third Psalm and a prayer that incorporated a lot of our feelings . . ."

"I had regarded religion in the time of crisis as just another prescription for crutches. I surprised myself at just how comfortably I used those crutches. Surrounded by other worshipers at a service, reciting traditional prayers, or singing in unison, it was comforting to find that when my faith was running low, I could turn to another faith which had stood the test of thousands of years. If that faith and the people who trusted in it had survived, then so would I."

By treating yourself well, you could become your own best friend. Not by becoming completely self-sufficient. Most of us are happier when we have someone with whom to share part of our lives. But by taking care of yourself and accepting yourself, you will be better able to cope with those moments of despair. You will recognize your strengths as well as your weaknesses. And you will become more confident that you can manage the challenging days ahead. After all, if you're not nice to yourself, who will be?

10. *Try to Turn Your Pain into a Positive Experience*

Death ends a life, not a relationship. Because of your painful separation, which is like an operation, there will always be scars.

As the scars become fainter, you are healing:

"I love being alive. My wife did lose the most by dying — and that makes me sad . . ."

"Even though my child died, I can't stop living . . ."

"The gift of life is still mine. Now is the time to start living again."

You are experiencing life in a context of new meanings and growth. In many a sigh is found an insight; in sorrow, a jolt out of complacency.

"Knowing love and adjusting to loss has made me a stronger person."

"The lessons of living learned from our child's joyous acceptance of her life help us with our other children. We never put off a thing we can do together — we may never have another chance."

"Through my grief, I have become a more sympathetic, stronger, and more capable person. I am kinder, have more understanding, and am more willing to hear (not just listen to) others; I know that the real healing process comes from within as I enlarge upon my strengths. I still don't know why my husband died, but I have learned to live more usefully and help others."

"I would truly listen to my patients and take the extra time to sit down now, knowing that tomorrow may be too late. I can say that the thing that carried me through was the ability to turn a painful and negative experience into something positive and creative."

Your loved one, now, lives in memory. In Dr. Elisabeth Kübler-Ross's words, you have the "ability to turn a painful and negative experience into something positive and creative." Resolve to live as your beloved would want you to live, love as they would want you to love, and serve others as they would have wanted you to serve. The Chinese word-picture symbol for *crisis* is the same as the symbol for *opportunity*. The Hebrew word for *crisis* is *mashber;* the same word refers to the travail of a woman in childbirth. Your crisis of death can give way to the birth of new ways of living without your loved one at your side — to do honor to his or her memory. This is your call to action. Death is a challenge to new life.

Weeping bitterly, mourning fully, pay tribute to sorrow, as he deserves, then compose yourself after your grief, for grief can bring on an extremity and heartache, destroy one's health. For him it was yesterday, for you it is today.
—Ecclesiasticus, 38:17

Seppli, a young man of twenty-eight years, died of cancer in Switzerland.

His sister-in-law, Dr. Elisabeth Kübler-Ross, "learned [her] lesson out of this pain," and became the foremost pioneer in the field of death and dying.

Dr. Kübler-Ross, psychiatrist and world-renowned authority on death, has traveled extensively and lectured widely. Her books are considered classics and have sold millions of copies. She now offers an intensely personal account of how she first became involved in a death-denying society.

HOW I BECAME INTERESTED IN DEATH AND DYING

BY ELISABETH KÜBLER-ROSS

One experience of death that affected me very deeply was the death of my most beloved brother-in-law, Seppli, who had been married to my triplet sister for only one year. He was a young man in his late twenties, a mountain climber and skier, who was always cheerful and loved his fellow man. Perhaps his most outstanding feature was his ever-present, big, happy, grin that made him one of the most sought-after friends for outings, for climbing and hiking, and sometimes for simply going up into the mountains to collect rocks and flowers.

He came from a simple family of many children and had learned early in life to share and to look at the sunny side of life. He had no great ambitions but was able to earn a very comfortable living for my sister and himself; they seemed to live in a constant honeymoon.

When he came to our house, he would play the guitar or the violin, and my sister would play the piano. We would sit for hours, singing songs together — from ballads to country songs to yodeling. And it seemed that every memory of his presence was filled with smiles and sunshine.

It was in early spring of my last year in medical school that he developed abdominal pains and eventually sought out medical help. His physician explained to him that he had a stomach ulcer and had to go on a very strict diet. Although he was an extremely good patient and followed instructions carefully, he went from bad to worse. His pains increased and he lost an enormous amount of weight. He looked very thin and ashen. The spark disappeared from his life.

It was during this time that I became aware of a very strong intuition that overcame all my scientific and intellectual thinking. I was convinced that my beloved brother-in-law did not have ulcers but that there was something much more seriously wrong with him.

As a medical student, my opinion was, naturally, not treasured by professional colleagues, who, insulted, wrote back that I could check the x rays myself if I had doubts about the diagnosis. And, indeed, his x rays showed classical stomach ulcers. Yet his whole clinical picture belied this diagnosis.

It was on impulse that I made a phone call to an out-of-town physician who was famous for his incredible skill in surgery, but at the same time was known as a most intuitive, sensitive, caring humanitarian. I shared with him my intuitive knowledge or fear, whichever it was, and asked him for a second opinion. He was most cordial. He not only evaluated my brother-in-law and gave him a thorough physical examination, but he accepted him for surgery and was most open and frank with me, telling me there was a slight possibility that he, indeed, had ulcers, but that underneath there might be something more seriously wrong.

In order to alleviate my anxiety, he invited me to scrub in during surgery and to witness the outcome of the operation firsthand. I was so convinced of my own impression that I prepared my sister gingerly for the possibility that her twenty-eight-year-old husband might have cancer. I told her I would attend the surgery, and that after the surgery I would give her an immediate phone call. If it was, indeed, bad news, I would simply tell her that I was right about my hunch.

I remember scrubbing into surgery. I remember standing on a footstool and watching the incision being made on my beloved friend's abdomen. I was most anxious when they went in and discovered a very widespread cancer of the stomach with some superimposed ulcerations that were the only visible part of the x ray. The kind elderly surgeon just looked at me over his horn-rimmed glasses with sadness and shook his head. He opened up the incision to show me the extensiveness of the cancer and then slowly and sadly and obviously with great love and compassion, closed up the wounds. My brother-in-law was wheeled out of the operating room into a private room, where I was allowed to sit and hold his hand.

I remember him, slowly coming out of the anaesthetic, looking at me with an almost forced, little grin, happy that he did not wake up alone, happy that someone was sitting there holding his hand.

It was only after he fully awoke that I left him to call my sister and give her the bad news. There was a silence at the other end of the phone. Later on, naturally, we talked about the possibility of spending those next few days together as much as would be humanly possible. Since my sister was working, she was not free during the daytime. I was in the midst of my final exams. There were too few moments that we could sit together and sing and share our feelings, our pain and also our joy.

My greatest pain came when I left my home town to take over a country practice quite far from Zurich. I bid good-bye to my family and my ailing, very thin and weakening brother-in-law. Shortly after I became established in my country practice, I woke up early one morning, as the waiting room bell continually rang, and my waiting room filled up with patients who wanted to be seen before they went to work. I had just put on my white coat to enter my office when the telephone rang, and Seppli, in a weak voice at the other end of the line, told me he was back in the hospital—that it would be lovely if I would come and visit with him, and that he really needed to talk to me.

My unfortunate early conditioning of being a reliable physician, of not keeping patients waiting, of always being there day and night, weekends and weekdays, prevented me from hearing the urgency of his plea. I told him I had a waiting room full of patients, but three days later I would take a weekend off, and drive to Zurich to visit him in the hospital. Seppli simply thanked me, accepting my choice, and hung up.

The next day while I was putting a sign out that my office would be closed on the weekend for family matters, the telephone rang. Seppli had died.

I was heartbroken that I had not responded to his last plea for help, that I was not able to hear him, that I did not remember the modesty of this beautiful man who had never asked for anything, ever. The only time he ever asked me for something, I postponed until it was too late.

I still remember driving to Zurich on the weekend in the drizzling rain, having found time to go to the funeral, but not having found time to talk to him when he needed to hear me and to talk to me. I remember the stories my sister told me that her husband, coming from a Catholic family, was refused the last rites because he had married a Protestant. I remember the stories of how he pleaded with three priests to be seen and to get the last unctions of the church in which he grew up. And all three of them turned their backs on him. He died with grief and guilt and in sadness that his last few pleas were not heard and responded to. We were also told that he could not be buried in a Catholic cemetery, but would be allowed to be buried outside the cemetery walls.

There was an incredible amount of unfairness in all these choices. In terms of practicing "Love thy neighbor as thyself," Seppli had probably been the best example of a Christian I have ever seen. He had never hurt a fly. He was an example of unconditional love and sunshine, yet he was refused help in the last few days of his life, at the time of his greatest anguish and suffering.

I returned to my country practice after the funeral. And I decided that I was going to learn my lesson out of this pain, that I was not going to allow the loss and grief to wear me down and drain my energy, but henceforth I would truly listen to my patients. And if someone said, "Sit down now," I would take the extra time to *sit down now,* knowing that tomorrow might be too late.

I also have had an opportunity to talk to hundreds and thousands of priests, Protestant ministers, and rabbis and share my experiences with them, pleading with them to help their fellow man and to stop the discrimination that was so dreadfully artificial and so unfair and also so un-Christian. Christ himself said "Love thy neighbor," but he didn't specify thy Jewish neighbor, thy Protestant neighbor, thy Catholic neighbor, thy white neighbor, thy black neighbor.

I am sure that the pain and the loss, the grief and the guilt over the death of Seppli, who was such an example of unconditional love, was one of the highest motivating forces, not only in making a compassionate, listening physician out of me, but in later leading me to work with dying patients and their families. Through his death and the pain and anguish of his last, lonely days he has indirectly touched thousands and thousands of dying patients all over the world. Looking back at this painful experience, I can say that the thing that carried me through was the ability to turn a painful and negative experience into something positive and creative.

WHAT HELPED
When a Child Dies

When a child dies, you lose your future.

In December 1976, Ann gave birth to a full-term stillborn baby boy. In what follows she tells about her experience. She and two other social workers, Jean Stringham and Judy Riley, have researched and written a paper entitled "Mourning a Stillborn Baby." They have presented their findings at several Boston-area hospitals in order to help sensitize health professionals to the unique problems of stillbirth. Ann's husband, Joseph, is a physician.

A STILLBIRTH

Talk to Your Family about Your Feelings

Death sometimes comes announced, as when a person dies after a serious illness. Sometimes it comes suddenly, when there is, for instance, an accidental death. With stillbirth, death comes suddenly and at a time when your hopes and excitement are at their highest.

I can remember my excitement as I woke our sons, Nicky, age seven, and Danny, age six, to tell them that I was in labor and the baby would be born soon. My husband Joe, and I bundled them up, took them to our next-door neighbors, and left for the hospital. This had been a perfect pregnancy, and now the baby was going to arrive right on the due date — December 12. The baby's room and clothes were all ready. I had hired a 12-hour-a-week baby-sitter so I could return to my part-time job after the holidays and keep up with my tennis. Most of all, I felt we had done the psychological work of getting ready for a third child. Three years before I had been pregnant for several months, but rather than a fetus making my stomach swell, it was a hydatiform mole, a pre-cancerous tumor of the placenta. My fears about all the blood loss, the prophylactic chemotherapy, and the constant testing for a recurrence had left me pretty conflicted about another pregnancy. But everything had been normal this time and I felt that soon I would be holding my baby.

I went into a labor room while Joe changed into a scrub suit. The nurse listened for the heartbeat in several different places. She left and returned with another nurse and some more instruments. When I asked about the heartbeat, they said that there was sometimes difficulty with the instruments. As the nurses moved faster, I became anxious, and when Joe came in dressed in his scrub suit, I started to cry and told him how worried I was. He told the nurses to call the doctor immediately. When the doctor arrived, he listened for the heartbeat and then said, "It doesn't look good. I am going to have to break your water." The look on his face as I felt the water gushing out told me the answer. "Is it stillborn?" I asked, and he nodded. As Joe and I cried, my first thought was that the baby was deformed in some way and that I was getting off easily by having it die now.

As I remember, the labor was not too bad. I had practiced natural childbirth exercises and had the satisfaction out of doing at least that right. I wanted to be awake and have Joe with me in the delivery room, but the doctor said that general anesthesia was better "in these cases." All my confidence and assertiveness gone, I agreed. When the anesthesiologist did not arrive in several minutes and pain became stronger, I said that I just wanted to push the baby out. The room was very quiet as the doctor caught the baby in some green surgical paper and put him in the corner of the room. When I asked, the doctor said it was a little boy. I knew I had to see the baby. I had to know that he wasn't another tumor.

After whispered consultation between the doctor and nurse, with several hurried peeks at the baby, they pulled back the paper so I could see. I saw a little boy, somewhat blue, who looked like our other sons at birth. Skin had sloughed off his stomach and he had some bruises. I didn't dare ask them to bring him over to me. Just letting me see him seemed like such a concession; they made me feel ghoulish. When Joe came into the delivery room, I told him it was a boy and asked if he wanted to see him. I was disappointed that he didn't want to.

I was taken to a private room on the maternity ward. There the reality of what had happened began to hit me. All those baby sounds were for the other mothers, not for me. It was morning and Joe had to go home to call my parents, his family, and, hardest of all, tell Nicky and Danny.

There was a phone in the room and I called a neighbor who had had a stillbirth several years before. I confided that I had insisted on seeing the baby. She said, "Not seeing my baby is my biggest regret." That made me feel better. Then I called Joe to find out about the boys' reactions. He said that the boys and the neighbors had a betting pool to guess the sex of the baby, and everyone was expecting him to declare the winners. Instead he had to tell them that the baby was dead. They were just stunned.

That afternoon Joe, my parents, Nicky and Danny came to the hospital. I was happy to see everyone, but the whole thing seemed like a dream. I told Nicky and Danny to be sure to tell their teachers and classmates about the baby the next day. I didn't want them to feel it was something they should hide. Joe came from the admitting office with the death certificate that said "Baby Boy Ross." We decided then that we would not name the baby because it would make us feel like we had really lost a baby rather than just a wish or a dream.

When I came home from the hospital a day and a half after the baby's birth there were flowers, plants, cards, letters, poems, food, and even whole meals. Many people had called and I was surprised to find out how fast the news spread. My parents were there to help out, and I had a lot of visitors to tell and retell about the baby's death. I was taken aback by people's kindness and concern. I felt guilty over the attention. I hadn't been able to sustain my baby's life. I felt I deserved public punishment rather than kindness. Things were so busy that there wasn't much time to think about the empty nursery.

The reality of losing the baby hit on the third day when my milk started to come in. I had been given pills to stop the milk, but they didn't work. I cried a lot and remembered nursing Nicky and Danny. I was in pain and I was angry. Why didn't my body know that the baby was dead?

The boys were solicitous the first few days. Then one day while we were making a puzzle together Nicky again asked why the baby had died. Trying to be patient, I said again that I didn't know. Nicky said, "It was because you played tennis too much. It was your fault." When I protested, he said that maybe it happened because I walked behind a car and breathed carbon monoxide, which didn't hurt me but went along that cord to the baby. In some ways, it felt good to have Nicky so openly angry with me. He was expressing a lot of my own guilty feelings.

Danny, on the other hand, seemed to reflect my sadness. He said, "Mom, I wish you had never gotten pregnant, because then I wouldn't be so disappointed now." Danny got reacquainted with his teddy bear. He played with it a lot and fed it with a white plastic bowling pin that looked like a baby bottle. At Christmas he hung up a stocking for the teddy bear.

There was the problem of what to do with the baby's body — still at the hospital morgue. Two days after I got home the pathologist called and said that the preliminary autopsy was completed but the cause of death was completely unknown; we would have to decide what to do with the body. Before this I had assumed that the hospital would take care of this and the call presented one more struggle. My father suggested that we donate the baby's body to a medical school. I felt terribly rejected when the pathologist called back after checking around, and said the medical schools had more than enough babies' bodies.

Our minister recommended a local undertaker and Joe went to the funeral home. I was prepared for a lot of expense and negotiations, and was surprised when Joe came home and said there was no charge. This undertaker did stillborn burials as a community service using the town plot, especially for stillbirths. Digging the grave — $25 — was the only cost. Joe told me about the little white box for the baby. He said it looked like something a fancy baby doll would come in.

At the end of the week the minister came to call. Things were awkward for a few minutes. Were we bereaved? Yes, but not in the usual way. We hadn't lost someone close to us — or had we? The minister assumed that we *had* lost someone and talking with him helped me cut through my denial. "A hundred years ago," he said, "stillbirths were more common and women knew how to react to the tragedy. We have lost the societal guidelines." His words helped me feel more comfortable about not knowing how to react. We decided that a graveside service would mean the most to us.

It was a cold, clear day, a week after the baby's death and a week before Christmas when we buried the baby. Just Joe, the undertaker, the minister, and I were at the cemetery. The minister read the Twenty-third Psalm and a prayer that incorporated a lot of the feelings we had expressed to him when he came to call. He said that as well as acknowledging our grief, we should be thankful for the family we did have. I was glad Joe had prepared me for how the little box would look. I could picture the baby lying in it. Joe was silently sobbing during the service and seemed to get more release from the ceremony than I did.

After the baby was buried, I felt I should go on with my life. I had two children, a nice home, husband, job, friends and family. I thought things would be as they were before I got pregnant. Professionally I knew about grieving, but I didn't want to believe that the process applied to stillbirth, or to me. I didn't know I would feel so sad for such a long time.

It was hard to tell the dozens of people who asked "Did you have a boy or girl" that the baby was stillborn. It was hard seeing little babies in stores or on home visits at work. The hardest to look at were the babies of friends who had been pregnant at the same time. I would never be a part of this newly formed peer group. I tried to keep very busy and kept hoping that the crying, dreams, and constant thoughts about the baby would stop.

About six months after the baby died, we took a month-long train trip to California for our summer vacation. We started planning the trip literally while I was still in the labor room. It was sort of a "sour grapes" reaction, talking about all the exciting things we would be able to do without a baby to tie us down. As the trip got closer, I became more depressed because what I really wanted was the baby, not the trip. It became very important to me to order the baby's grave marker before we left so that if something happened to all of us at least there would be some proof that the baby had existed. The trip to California turned out well. It was a time of enjoying our family the way it was rather than wishing it was something more.

A few months after the baby died, one of my co-workers mentioned that she had started writing a paper about stillbirth several years before but had put it aside because it was so depressing. She was interested in the subject because her older sister had had a stillbirth many years ago. Although her sister had three other children after the stillbirth, my friend thought that she had never really resolved the loss. We brought in another friend who was interested in issues of loss and grieving; together the three of us did a research project on mourning a stillborn baby. The weekly meetings during the two years of this project were very therapeutic. These were times when I could talk over my feelings with friends. It was like a self-help group for me. Interviewing other women who had had stillbirths, hearing similarities to my own feelings, and trying to help them helped me.

What is life like now three and a half years later? I still feel sad about the baby from time to time, especially around the time of his birthday. I think of him now not as "Baby Boy Ross" but as Alexander Joseph Ross, the name we had chosen before his birth. Because of our ages I don't think I should get pregnant again; I couldn't stand another loss. I've taken my winnings, my two sons and my relationship with my husband, and walked away from the table. In some ways I feel the pressure to be a "Super-Mom" to the boys. I try to be there when they come home from school, and I hate to miss any of their sports matches. I occasionally toy with the idea of adopting an older child, but I wonder if that would upset the balance that our family has now.

My husband's comments:

Our excited trip to the hospital when Ann was in labor, the shock at our baby being dead, the painful sharing with our boys and family, the burial service, and the immediate mourning we did together. Then our mourning often diverged. I wondered at times about Ann spending so many hours thinking about it. Although I had experienced profound grief, it was not something I continued to dwell on. But for months, each time the subject of the baby came up, Ann cried and seemed almost tortured. I wanted to comfort her, but I also wished that she had more distance from it. Maybe it is rationalization, but perhaps pregnancy is something a man does not participate in so much. It is nine months when a woman is intensely involved in a way the man is not, so the sense of failure and disappointment may not hit him so hard.

Now, three years later, the loss for me has become a deep sadness along with some other losses I have experienced. I feel both guilty and relieved that Ann has found some other ways to express her grief and other people with whom to share it. The professional paper about stillbirth she has written with her colleagues is very moving and will be instructive to others. Reconsidering and writing down our experience has helped us do some further grief work together.

Ann Ross

Cara was born six or seven weeks prematurely. She had problems with her heart, with breathing, and with massive bleeding and infection. Cara lived for five days and died on January 24, 1978, in Iowa City, Iowa. She lived long enough for her mother to see and touch her.

Her mother, Colleen Butler, a pediatric nurse practitioner, is now working with countless families who have suffered the death of a child.

Each year in this country approximately 35,000 newborn infants die. This cold statistic translates into an enormous collection of human suffering for surviving parents, siblings, and the greater circle of family and friends.

A BABY LIVES FIVE DAYS

Counseling May Be the Answer

For five years, we have worked on perfecting our love. The perfect expression of our love has been the birth of our daughter on January 18, 1978. Cara Aileen was a beautiful child with curly brown hair, a cute nose and even the Finan toe! She lived until her mother was able to see and touch her. Cara died Tuesday morning, January 24, 1978, peacefully and quietly — having brought us joy, happiness, and completeness as a family.

— Cara's birth announcement

Monday, November 28, 1977

Another month gone! Weight gain — 16 lbs.; baby — active; tummy — full. Mom feels great! People I work with daily exclaim how I have "popped out" or "bloomed"; people whom I do not see very often are surprised at how "little" my tummy is, considering the fact that I am in my seventh month of pregnancy. I know that I am beginning to walk more like a pregnant lady. No doubt about the protruding stomach.

Christmas Day, 1977

During our meal of stuffed cornish hen, champagne, and apple pie, Frank brought out a wishbone. I could not think of anything to wish for, so we couldn't pull! We realize that we are coming to the close of a special time of our marriage and that our child will bring new dimensions. Frank really enjoyed the baby last night. "Thumper" was very active and Frank didn't miss a movement.

Friday, January 5, 1978

I had an appointment with Dr. Crane. There was some edema — swelling of the fingers, ankles, and eyelids.

Friday, January 13, 1978

I've been having headaches. Dr. Crane found that I still had protein in my urine, swelling, and that my blood pressure was elevated. Obviously, he said, the diuretic had not been effective, so I should discontinue using it, go home immediately, and be on complete bed rest. If things were not improved by my return Monday, we would consider hospitalization.

Wednesday, January 18, 1978

It is difficult to report these things because I do not have
any recollection of them happening. Apparently a Cae-
sarean section was performed and they found an added
complication. Every time they tried to separate the placenta from the uterus there was a lot of bleeding. This
rare condition, placenta accreta, means that the placenta
has grown into the uterine wall. So it was necessary to do
a hysterectomy. A four-pound ten-ounce girl was born.
Cara was transferred to the tertiary center in Iowa City,
sixty miles away.

I was given five units of blood and sent to the intensive
care unit. My girlfriend Maureen and Frank contacted
my family. Mother, Dad, and my sister Kitty flew out from
Michigan immediately. The five of them kept a constant
vigil, always there during the five-minute visiting periods.
Four days later, I was transferred back to the maternity
ward. Frank, Mother, and Dad visited Cara in Iowa City
and took pictures of her. They kept me informed of how
she was doing.

Monday, January 23, 1978

I received a call from Dr. Kelly who had been working
with the baby. We had come to a point of having to make
a decision. Did we want to keep up with the aggressive
measures? We both knew that we did not want aggressive
measures to continue. What we really wanted was for me
to get a chance to see the baby and we did not know how
to do that. In the end, it was worked out that I would go
by ambulance to Iowa City, be admitted as a patient and
finish my treatment there. It was understood that I would
not be able to see the baby because I had an elevated

temperature and probably an infection. I would not be allowed in the nursery, but perhaps something could be worked out so that I could see the baby as soon as possible after she died. Dr. Kelly said he was not going to be on duty that night but he would write an order to the effect that as soon as she died, all the tubes would be pulled, and she would be wrapped up and brought to me so I could see her. It was the best he could do and he didn't know if that order would be honored or if it would be superseded by the administration.

The ambulance arrived. Sue, one of the nurses, accompanied me. Earlier she had let me know she understood some of what I was experiencing because she had been in a similar situation with her baby about a year ago; she had lost her baby and was unable to have any more children. She was very empathetic and supportive.

Now she let me talk until I was too tired to talk anymore. Then we sat in silence for a while.

When I arrived in Iowa City, I was very demanding of Frank. I kept saying, "Is she alive or is she dead?" I was too anxious to understand what he was saying. As it turned out, the nurses who were taking care of Cara made every effort to try to have me see her while she was still living. They put her into an incubator and used a hand ventilator rather than a respirator so that I would have a chance to see her. Two nurses and a Dr. Evans brought the baby in in an incubator. I put my hands through the portholes of the incubator and I got to see and feel my daughter for the first time.

Cara was soft and warm. She did not respond to my touch. She was just barely living. I couldn't see very well so I don't know what color she was, but Frank said she was pale, bordering on yellow. Her skin was swollen and stretched, but she was still living. She had a chest tube in and a tube in her mouth and they were ventilating for her. I was able to run my hand over her stomach and her chest, to feel her legs, to look at her toes and her fingers. I opened her eyes and felt her forehead and her head. She was just beautiful. She did not seem to have any birthmarks on her at all, which I thought she would have had. Her skin was clear and soft. She had a beautiful nose.

I could not believe the joy that I felt inside me — the completeness that I felt as a mother, which I hadn't been able to feel before I had seen her. She brought life to me, like a candle had been lit inside me once I was able to feel her. I could feel my stitches, I could feel my intestines, I could feel my heart opening up. She was just beautiful. She was warm, she was alive, and she was mine.

Then they took her away. I felt such a happiness. I was just glowing. It was one of the happiest days of my life. I felt like this was Cara's birthday because I got to see her; even though I knew she was dying. I called home so I could share my happiness with Kitty, Mother, and Dad. The nursery nurse came in before she left for home to see if there was anything else she could do. I assured her that she had helped more than I had ever hoped for by letting me see my baby while she was still living. Frank left at about 11:00 that night and found a hotel room. He received a call about 2:30 A.M. and he came to the hospital and told me that Cara was dead.

I was still glowing from having seen her. I can't remember my reaction. A short time later, a mortician came in and had us sign papers to allow a postmortem on her and to permit us to donate her body to the university. He said that probably they would be able to use her body for anatomical study and that after a month she would be cremated and that if any time before then we decided to change our minds, we were welcome to receive her body. Dr. Evans came in to see if we had any questions. He left and we closed the door, pulled the curtain, and Frank crawled into bed with me. We stayed together from about 3:30 until 6:30 in the morning. The nurses did not disturb us at all. When the night nurse finally did come in about 6:45 A.M. to take my temperature, Frank got up and left.

Tuesday, January 31, 1978

These things I know: The past two to three weeks have brought many changes; people have been very, very good to us. We have gotten cards and letters and calls from so many people — everyone expressing love and concern and support. I know that I was pretty out of it for a week; I am not really sure what happened except for what people have filled me in on and I have tried to put these things down. I know that I lost contact with my body and with my baby. I know that I am forever grateful to all the people who have helped us. I miss Cara very much.

I still cannot believe she is gone and it is all over. I know that I am really going to miss Mother. She is leaving in the morning. I am almost afraid to be alone — to be with my thoughts — but it is probably what I need to do. I feel as if I do not know my own capabilities or my limitations and I am frightened. I really don't understand what is going on. Mother keeps my spirits up; she gives me love and life and support. When she leaves, I am going to have to find those things within me. I pray that I can.

Tuesday, February 7, 1978

We had a very good session with Chaplain Williams. We talked again about the fact that Frank and I are mourning so differently. Chaplain Williams pointed out that we were "searching out" our feelings; that even though our emotions were very different we were still very much the same in our searching out process. We were able to see how we are tending to recycle our feelings of guilt, of anger, of depression and how they come out in different forms. The message that kept coming out during the session was that we are having normal reactions. Chaplain Williams was able to show us how we have been changing with each visit. The most important thing is that the two of us are communicating. The conversation shifted from just discussing Cara and the grieving process to also discussing me. I was feeling guilty that I am always taking care of myself and working on my physical recuperation rather than dealing with Cara and her loss and the meaning of her in our lives. I felt that I was focusing too much on myself. I am learning many things through this experience — about dealing with my patience, or my impatience; dealing with the authority role, with being a patient; dealing with grief.

Thursday, February 9, 1978

We went to the Horsleys' in the evening and had home-made ice cream. Shortly before we were supposed to leave, I started talking with Frank about what I was feeling and had a good cry. We talked about Cara. Frank was very gentle. When we have discussions like this, they turn out to be a very rich experience for me. I'm afraid it made us about an hour late for the Horsleys'. Somehow it is difficult to program emotions for the right time.

Monday, February 13, 1978

I will never cease to be amazed at how people find out about Cara and at what their reactions are. People that

I hardly even know have been writing and calling — people that I haven't heard from or talked to for a long time. How does the word spread? I want very much to write to people to let them know how much I appreciate their reaching out to us. Frank and I have written a card that, hopefully, will serve as a birth announcement, death announcement, and thank you card all in one.

Tuesday, April 4, 1978

I have not done much writing since making the tape after Cara's death. I have done a lot of searching, reading, thinking, some doing, very little crying.

I have found that people are sincerely interested in how I am doing; not just in verbiage. And when they ask, I tell them that I am doing well. But tonight I am alone. Tonight I read material on Sudden Infant Death Syndrome. It reopened some very frail scars; reaffirmed that grieving does not end. It reemphasized that I am not the only human being who has experienced the death of an infant. It showed me that others who have lost loved ones can reach out to others — to me — and can help. I see that I am normal in what I am experiencing.

Obviously I must still be searching because I find myself gravitating toward books on death, articles on grieving, conferences on dying.

I wonder if the emptiness I feel is accentuated by the fact that the loss was so sudden, so unannounced, and so final. I wonder if I will ever begin to realize that my pregnancy is over and Cara is gone. I wish I could talk with someone, share what I am feeling. So many people have offered and keep making contacts, and yet there is nothing to say. It comes in waves. People love me and offer me their support but they cannot understand; I cannot understand. There is bewilderment and emptiness. How can this be? It has been too many weeks for these types of feelings to be here; and to be here with such strength. It is good for me to write. I feel much better now.

Wednesday, May 10, 1978

Mother's Day is approaching — my first. It makes me hurt and cry. I want Cara. I want to be a normal child-bearing woman. I want the trials and tribulations, the joys of raising my child. I am so glad that I have my work; that I can be with the children and their mothers. But I am feeling jealous — jealous of women who can bear children. I want my own child, here, now, living. Why does there have to be a Mother's Day?

Saturday, July 29, 1978

Almost two months have passed since the last entry. I have gone to a grief recovery group with Chaplain Williams a few times. I think there could be a more effective group for bereaved parents, but this is the closest I can come for the moment. I read an article written by a mother who lost twins. The grieving period was aptly described and her recovery has been similar to mine. I think the main work is over. The low times are few and far between and it is not as difficult to recover.

Friday, August 25, 1978

I just reread the journal about Cara — so thankful I was able to keep it — rereading about what went on brings back the power and the beauty of the whole experience. Seems so long ago; I had forgotten the intensity. Reading and rereading the diary has been such an effective grieving tool for me.

Saturday, December 2, 1978

Christmas is coming quickly. I look forward so to having children. We plan to adopt. It's hard to believe that Cara would be almost a year old now. It would be her first Christmas. Guess that dates me as a mommy!

Pat Dicken is starting back to work. Her little girl is two months old now. I am still amazed that people can have pregnancies successfully, that the pregnancy can go to full term and the baby can survive, indeed thrive, for two months. I thank God that such a miracle is possible.

Knowing that I will never again be able to wear maternity clothes, to have my abdomen expand, and to successfully bring a full-term healthy baby into our family makes me that much more impatient to get on with the adoption process so we can have a family with children. There is no possibility, with the present state of medicine, that we can procreate, so I want to move on, not stand still anymore. I am so impatient.

One would think that I would have learned the lesson of patience this past year. Obviously I'm doomed to have that be a lifelong lesson, a task that is extremely difficult for me.

Friday, January 18, 1980

Today is Cara's second birthday. This morning I received a call from Rabbi Grollman, asking me if I would send a condensed version of my diary to be part of his book. What a neat way to be able to celebrate Cara's birthday, by sharing it with others. But first I must attend to the crying of my two sons, Brian, age three months, and Sean, age two months!

Colleen Butler

On July 10, 1965, Lawrence Anthony, age three months, died of an illness that had no name. Today, it is known as Sudden Infant Death Syndrome (SIDS).

His mother, Carolyn Szybist, a registered nurse, has devoted her professional life to the National Sudden Infant Death Syndrome Foundation as its executive director. She coordinates volunteer activities for chapters throughout the United States.

Sudden Infant Death Syndrome (SIDS or "crib death") is the unexpected death of a child in apparently good health. Typically the baby is between one month and seven months, although SIDS can strike from one- or two-day-old babies to five- or six-year-old children. Usually the baby is put to bed without any suspicion of anything out of the ordinary. Sometime later, a few minutes, several hours, the following morning, the infant is found lifeless. There is no outcry, no apparent struggle. No one knows the cause. No one is to blame. It is a disease of exclusion. When the physician rules out every possible cause for the seemingly healthy baby's death, it is called SIDS. One in every five hundred live births ends in a Sudden Infant Death Syndrome.

A SUDDEN INFANT DEATH

Find a Friend Who Cares

Mrs. Judith Lovell
Northbrook, Illinois

Dear Judy,

Somewhere in the many speeches that I have given about Sudden Infant Death Syndrome, I have wanted to use your name, almost as if it could become a scientific

44

reference. But I haven't, and I rarely talk about you when I talk about SIDS, because you share one of those personal places in my heart that is more easily felt than spoken of.

When I look back over the fourteen years since Larry died, and remember that time, I don't think of you immediately. You weren't there in my house when he died. You weren't at the funeral. You weren't one of the first people I thought I needed to talk to. But when I was asked who helped me the *most*, with my grief, and with the crisis of the death of my tiny son, with my fears, with my guilt, with my survival, there is only one good answer. You.

How do I explain what you did, through your presence and your friendship, that got me out of the black awful pit of grief and out where the sunshine could find me? How do I define your patience? How do I tell anyone that you utilized *yourself* to help me? Yours are not the skills that can be taught; they are simply real human qualities that defy naming or explaining. Grief is such a long, ugly journey. Helping me must have seemed endless although I never heard you complain. I needed someone with patience and compassion and time — and you gave me all of that.

Do you realize that we really didn't know each other very well at the time that Larry was born? We used to talk at work when I was pregnant, but aside from that, we were little more than "employment" acquaintances. Sometime after Larry was born, you called me at home and asked me to a Tupperware party at your house, so that I could see some of the people again and escape diapers for a few hours. And it was because of that party that you came to my house on a warm, July afternoon to deliver the Tupperware and to chat. You were addicted to babies, I recall. You spent much of the afternoon rocking Larry and cuddling him and talking about having another baby.

Two days later, my son was dead, suddenly, unexpectedly. You had known him because of that warm afternoon. I remember your telephone call of disbelief, when you learned from others about Larry. You used to call me from time to time after that, to talk about him, or just to talk. You usually knew when I needed someone; your ability to catch me at the right time was uncanny. But that isn't what you did to help, exactly, and I'm not sure I can explain it now, although I've tried.

When the world went away after the funeral and left me alone in my grief, you didn't. I asked everyone to leave me alone, and you pretended to listen. But your actions were warmly devious.

Do you recall that you never phoned and asked me if I wanted to go somewhere, or to ask if I was interested in taking my small daughter and your small girls out for the day? You knew I would say no. That is what I said to everyone else. What you did was give me a different option. Your calls always went something like this: "When we go to the zoo with the girls on Friday, do you want to bring the hot dogs or the Cokes?" And while I made the decision of which item, you removed me from the house. Your tactics were so highly sophisticated that I missed them, and I delight in remembering your warm management of the person I was in my grief.

In the cool days of autumn, when it seemed sacrilegious to think about celebrating anything, including Christmas, it was you who brought trunkloads of toy and gift catalogues to my house. And we pored over them as *you* decided what you would buy for your girls and I got caught in your plans.

It was you who always had time to talk on the telephone on rainy or dreary days. It was you who would talk to me when I worried irrationally about my daughter's health, fearful that she, too, would die.

It was you, too, who invited me to spend the entire day at your house on the date that would have been Larry's first birthday. You knew I couldn't spend that day in my house, and you coped with me for hours.

I don't recall that you ever lectured me, or chided me, or even kidded me about my irrational fears. You never made me feel that I was taking and not giving; you let the friendship be equal. I knew that I needed your calm strength, but you never made me feel like I was imposing, or taking. I never felt I had to apologize for my humanness, although I must have been oppressive at times.

But perhaps one of the finest gifts came in an unknowing way. For it was you who removed the last of my superstitious fears several years after Larry's death. When you became pregnant with your long-awaited son, you called me and asked if you could borrow Larry's crib. You did it casually and comfortably, knowing that the crib was in my attic and that I regarded it as almost an evil instrument of death. My mind saw the silliness of throwing it away, but my emotions could not deal with using it. And because of you, some months later I was able to put my own new baby in that crib without a thought, for the images had been replaced with your son, thriving, growing, and living.

I needed, ultimately, to learn all there was to learn about SIDS. And I needed to work through my guilt and my fears in my own way. No one could do that for me. But you read the information with me, and listened as I grew in my comprehension.

What you did was fill in those huge moments when information has nothing to do with humanness and fear. With every step I tried to take backward, you were gently tugging me forward. And when I failed in my great efforts at courage, and let the fear envelop me, you waited and simply cared.

Our lives have taken different paths now and we seldom see each other. But I don't feel removed from you in the warm recesses of my heart. It doesn't take being together to experience or remember friendship. You not only shared one of the terrible moments of my life, you made the difference in my moving ahead and living.

I can't teach what you did for me. But I can extend the spirit of your caring into how I help others, and that is a treasured gift in itself. I'm not certain that I ever realized at the time how important you were. And I am pretty certain that you didn't know either.

The greatest compliment I can pay you, all these years later, is to fervently hope that for every person in grief, there is a Judy.

Love,
Carolyn Szybist

On June 22, 1936, Edgar D. Jackson, aged fourteen months, died as the result of an accident.

His father, Reverend Edgar N. Jackson, is an eminent Methodist clergyman, specializing in the area of crisis intervention. In his many volumes one finds a most integrated study of the theological, psychological, and philosophical dimensions of bereavement.

Dr. Jackson now lives in Corinth, Vermont, where his time is devoted principally to writing, lecturing, and farming.

If children are born healthy, parents expect them to live for many years and outlive them. The sudden unanticipated death of a child requires a major psychological readjustment. There is no time to prepare for the tragic loss. Following a fatal accident the overwhelming feelings of shock, disbelief, and guilt are more intense than the reactions to an expected death. One parent may blame the other. "Our child has done nothing to deserve this" adds to the families' anger, bewilderment, and frustration. Grief feelings should never be delayed or repressed. Sometimes they need to be talked through; sometimes they are best felt in silence.

AN ACCIDENTAL DEATH

Don't Be Afraid of Silence

Maybe it wasn't an hour. It could have been forty-five minutes. But it has lasted almost half a century. For quality and for meaning nothing has surpassed it.

It happened like this. Estelle and I were young and filled with expectations about life. We were filled with pride and joy for our first-born. He was beautiful. He was intelligent. He was a fun-loving, joy-filled youngster, the kind that brings a rare form of delight to young parents. He was happy in the love that greeted him on entry upon the human scene. It seemed nothing could mar this idyllic scene.

Then it happened, unexpectedly and ruthlessly. An accident. Anxious hours in the hospital. Painful pacing and vain hope. The wounds were too great. His organs failed. Denials that rejected reality. Then kindly doctors with sad countenances saying, "We are so sorry ... we tried our best ... it wasn't good enough."

Reentry into a house so strangely silent. Retreat to the family room with tears and sorrows unrestrained. The flood of questions unanswered and unanswerable. How could it be? Why us? Where's justice in this world?

The doorbell sounded. Who could this be? Now, of all times? We want to be alone. We don't dare to be alone. Oh God, speak to us in our confusion!

I answered the door. A gray-haired clergyman from a neighboring church stood before me, eloquent tears in his eyes. He said nothing, but he took my hand with both of his. When I asked him to come in, he followed me silently.

Invited to sit down, he did so placing his elbows on his knees and his head in his hands, saying nothing. Every few minutes he would look at me sitting nearby and shake his head again with a burden of sadness moving over his countenance. He seemed at times to be in silent prayer, but no word gave a clue.

He communicated with pure and uncontaminated feeling, with perfect resonance to my sorrow. Yet in his silence he helped to articulate my impacted feeling. He shared my sorrow with the fullness of his being.

After a long time that was really short, or maybe it was a short time that had a mystical dimension, he stood up slowly, embraced me leaving some of his tears upon my cheek, and walked toward the door as if his feet were heavy. Again he took both of my hands in his and walked away having said not a word. I knew and trusted him so fully. He felt that no words could carry his feeling to my aching soul. None were needed. Deep spoke unto deep.

Forty-four years have passed since that quiet hour. They have illuminated my life. They have helped me understand Job and his silent friends. They have taught me not to be afraid of silence, but rather to understand its eloquence. In the many language forms we employ it is not unusual for words to clutter the potential for rebound of person to person. Words can get in the way and be misunderstood. Or their inadequacy becomes apparent to those who speak and those who listen. In rural Vermont, there is an expression for it: "Don't ruin the silence unless you can improve on it."

Grief is an emotion. Words tend to be intellectualizations. As one who has spent a lifetime using the spoken and written word, I hope for their usefulness. As one who has known sorrow, I have learned that there are times when the best of life is in the silence that needs no words.

My quiet friend was a master of erudite speech. He could move crowds with his verbal skill. Yet I remember him not for his words but for the warmth of spirit that knew when it was possible and necessary to move into higher levels of communication. His quiet hour then and now and many times in between has nourished my soul and led me to trust the healing power of the muted forms of speech that are best heard in silence.

Edgar N. Jackson

At the age of twenty months Kathleen was diagnosed with acute leukemia. She died on July 14, 1970, at the age of four years.

Her mother, Grace Powers Monaco, is a founding parent of Candlelighters, an international organization for parents of children and adolescents with cancer. She is president of Candlelighters Foundation, the information, education, and support mechanism for all Candlelighters parents groups. An attorney, she specializes in health and energy law.

Even though parents may have already suspected it, given the diagnosis of a fatal illness in their child, they still experience the initial feelings of shock and disbelief. There is often an intellectual admission of the reality; less frequently, an emotional acceptance. Despite the fact that death has been anticipated, the grief process does not end with the funeral. When death occurs, the family may be so physically weakened, that they are ill-prepared to begin the task of mourning and rebuilding their lives. It is not a sign of weakness to express the pain of separation — even after a lingering illness. Rather it is a step toward acceptance and ultimate recovery from grief.

WHEN A CHILD DIES FROM CANCER

Rejoice in Times Shared

Such a very small package to be carrying such a very large problem. A tiny girl — all dimples and teeth and dark curls and chubby legs. Diagnosed with acute lymphocytic leukemia at age twenty months. By almost four she had few dark curls left (radiotherapy), a bloated, blotchy, bruised body (chemotherapy/immunosuppressive drugs) — but the smile and the sparkle behind the eyes, the things that were really Kathleen Rea were still there. She was in her first relapse, on the way to a second remission. We were almost ready to bring her home from the hospital when her temperature suddenly shot up. By the time the offending bacteria was isolated, it was too late to stem the tide of infection.

"Mommy, I'm not coming home." "Why not, Kathleen?" "My machinery is all worn out." "If you don't come home where will you go?" "To heaven." "I'll miss you very much, Kathleen."

All the family members were called to see Kathleen. She stayed alert and without pain until she slipped into a coma about four hours before she died.

Two things I did not find helpful at the hospital: There was a lack of privacy for the terminal family. The appendectomy children shared the same floor. We appeared to be a bit of a freak show for the others. Game-playing — another burr in my saddle. A well-meaning new resident read Kathleen's chart, told us she was doing fine and we would have her home soon. Anyone with eyes, anyone who could read, knew she was dying.

She died in my arms with my father and a favorite aunt in attendance. There was relief with the grief. She had been through so much: Now she was at rest. But what a loss — the special sparkle of her personality. Her friend and brother would miss her with a keenness even beyond that her parents felt. David (then two) took and slept with Kathleen's giant Easter bunny until he was seven. He gave it up on the same day he talked to a close friend, a girl in his class, about his sister who died.

Our neighbors didn't ask what they could do — they simply *did*. Hams, soups, baked goods, provisions for those who would be attending Kathleen's funeral. Her coffin was closed with her picture on top. We shunned the extreme cosmetic artifices of death.

What carried us through? Families of Candlelighters. An organization composed of people like a great tall Irishman and his wife, my special listeners from Virginia. During Kathleen's illness and after her death, I was the cause of numerous sore ears from long telephone conversations. Early in treatment other parents helped me understand that Kathleen's cancer was no one's fault, that no guilt need be carried. I learned to rejoice in the beauty of time shared. I sat in my rocking chair and rocked and cried. Kathleen's cup was full before mine. She went before me to a place where we all in time must follow. Her death gave me a new purpose — to form parent support networks to help during good times, uncertain times, and bad; to put my energies behind the efforts to find cures or controls for cancer; and to improve the information available to families. Kathleen's light went out, but she lives on in all that we do for her memory. The lessons of living learned from her joyous acceptance of the limitations on her life help us with our other children. We never put off a thing we can do together. We may not have another chance.

It took six months before I could remember how beautiful she was; six months before I could remember her as anything but the bruised, blotchy, bloated body that housed her in her last weeks; six months before her spirit broke through to my memory and let me feel and sense her beauty again. I miss her very much. I think of her with love and tears. I cannot go to children's funerals anymore.

Now, ten years later, I still have trouble keeping my composure at the "remember the faithful departed" in church. Kathleen was open and demanded openness from those around her. Somehow I think she would not be displeased at my tears. Nor at my memory of her as a beautiful, brassy, bossy lady who is preparing a place for us in her company.

Grace Powers Monaco

Diana Gabrielle, almost ten years old, was killed instantly in a car accident in which her mother was also injured.

Two years after her death, in October 1972, her mother, Paula Shamres and her father, Arnold, founded the first American chapter of the Society of Compassionate Friends, an international support group for bereaved parents.

In 1968, Reverend Simon Stephens, a young Anglican priest, was assigned as chaplain at the Coventry & Warwickshire Hospital in England. Many children were dying in the hospital from illness and accidents. When they died, there was little care or attention paid to the bereaved parents.

On one occasion, when two boys had died on the same day, the bereaved parents met, and found that by sharing their grief in mutual understanding, they both were more able to cope with the traumatic shocks of the events.

These parents asked Reverend Stephens to help them form an organization that would offer friendship and understanding to all bereaved parents, thus the Compassionate Friends began. Since that time, chapters have been formed in England and around the world.

The Society of Compassionate Friends offers no shortcuts to the resolution of grief, but offers comfort at a time of agony and the consolation of a confidence that the bereaved family can turn its tragedy into a meaningful experience of understanding and growth.

A TEN-YEAR-OLD IS KILLED

Reach Out to Heal Yourself

It was Thursday, October 8, 1970, at 1:25 in the afternoon. On this warm south Florida day, my daughter Gabi, just twenty days from her tenth birthday, and I were just three blocks from our home on our way to a shopping center. As we approached the railroad crossing, I remember hearing Gabi say from the back seat of the car, "Go ahead, Mommie, it's all right." I laughed to myself thinking she was too little to be a back seat driver. Seconds later, as we crossed, the train hit us broadside at seventy-nine miles an hour.

I opened my eyes in the intensive care unit. My husband, Arnold, and my two sons, Jonathan and Seth, were standing at my bedside. Unaware of the bandages covering my head and the tubes in my body, I saw their faces through the numbness of sedation, and somehow I knew. "Where is Gabi? Where is my baby?" I cried. With tears in his voice, Arnold said, "We're your babies now."

They had buried my daughter on the eve of Yom Kippur, the Day of Atonement, while I fought for my life.

In the days that followed I began the long process of healing from the triple concussion, severe scalp lacerations, and from emergency abdominal surgery to remove my ovaries, which had been crushed by the steering wheel of my car. For the several weeks I was in the hospital, I was hazy from sedation. In my haziness one day, I removed all my tubes and was found in the closet trying to pack a bag to go home. The tubes were replaced and I was given nurses around the clock, because the doctors suspected that I was suicidal.

Later, I would realize that the physical discomfort of those weeks had been just the beginning of an emotional anguish that was to overcome me.

The emptiness was so painful when I arrived home; our boys were back at college, and there was no more Gabi. At first we were surrounded by relatives and friends and allowed every expression of grief. That first week there were so many visitors and phone calls. I made only one call, to my dearest cousins, David and Glory Kleiner, who had, some years earlier, been anguished by the loss of two daughters to cystic fibrosis. David was a doctor: to be one and not be able to help your own children had always seemed to me to be the most vile of agonies. David told me to take only one minute, one hour, one day at a time to cope with the miserable constant gut pain. His was the only really meaningful advice I received from any professional because, I would realize later, as a bereaved parent, he had been there. David, Glory, and their sweet daughter, Wendy, had survived their tragedies. I didn't know it at the time, but the seed of what I would come to know as Compassionate Friends was being planted in our lives even then.

Mary, a wonderful compassionate nurse, helped me through the first two weeks at home. Because I was unable to eat or to sleep very well, the doctors had prescribed tranquilizers and antidepressants. When Mary realized I was allergic to these crutches, she asked my doctors to substitute a drink or two before dinner and a sedative at bedtime. She helped me to give Gabi's clothes and possessions to my sister's little girls and friends, and she gently nudged me back behind a wheel, joking that she was protected because she was insured.

But Mary left; the visitors and phone calls slowed down and Arnold and I learned that we had to cry alone and help one another by pulling and tugging ourselves out of the deep pit of depression that often overwhelmed us. At times neither one of us could help when we were both down, but somehow there was always another tomorrow. We soon realized, though, that for some reason we were losing contact with friends and relatives. It seemed that people just couldn't face our loss with us. They didn't know what to say or do so they spoke to us in platitudes. "You were lucky she died instantly." "It was God's will."

"Time heals all wounds." "I know how you feel." We were saddened and angry to be "consoled" so, but it was worse still to be left alone.

When I called friends or relatives, they would have "other plans." We were alone for our twenty-fifth wedding anniversary. The waiters at the restaurant sang "Happy Anniversary" to us, and later we cried alone again. For my fiftieth birthday, Arnold made a party and invited people, but only a few came. Perhaps we grew closer as "two against the world," but it was so lonely a time. We were terribly hurt by this "conspiracy of silence" and we wondered what we had done to deserve such punishment. First a tragedy, then exile.

I was very close to my sister, Audrey, but it became apparent that even she could not cope. She felt guilty for not allowing Gabi to play at her home that fateful day because her children had had colds. Once she said that she should have let her in; she might have caught a cold, but at least she'd be alive. Another time her guilt and grief took a different tack. She blurted out that she had done me the biggest favor of my life by burying my daughter (she had the Shiva, the seven-day period of formal mourning, in her home).

After she said this, I left her home in a daze and drove to the shopping center where I noticed a white wall with nothing between me and it. I revved the motor and, my mind a blank, started moving toward it. A moment of madness! As I drove, a little old lady carrying two shopping bags stepped off the curb on my right. Despite my constant questioning of why I lived and my daughter died, my guilt at being a survivor as well as an instrument of my daughter's death, and my sister's words being still fresh in my mind, I suddenly discovered that I *do* "brake for little old ladies." I wondered if it was true that we all have jobs to do on earth. Gabi's was finished; mine wasn't.

But what was it to be? I looked into the gray heavens and asked for answers. Without hearing any, I somehow decided that the direction of my life was in God's hands.

I was estranged not only from my sister, Audrey, but also from our youngest son, Seth, for quite some time after the tragedy. Seth and I had had an argument just one month before the accident; the lingering hurt of that argument was now compounded by terrible guilt feelings. Sometime after the funeral, he asked my sister, "Did my mother try to commit suicide because of our argument?" Her answer was vehement. "Your mother would never try to commit suicide, especially with Gabi in the car." Pain and anguish had affected every member of our family, each in a different way.

Our religious faith faltered. To me God had been love, peace, wisdom, and beauty, all good things. But how could God give me a daughter after eleven years of waiting and then take her back at this tender age? If there was a God, he was an Indian giver!

For some time I met with a psychologist. He never told me I was going through a normal process of grief; and I thought I was losing my mind! He arranged for me to spend a night in a real "cuckoo's nest" so that I would see the difference. Despite "seeing the difference," I was still in agony.

Then, in May of 1971, after traveling a seemingly endless road of guilt, anguish, grief, and bereavement, Arnold came home one day with an article from *Time* magazine. It was about an organization founded in England to help bereaved parents. The article explained how Simon Stephens, an Anglican priest and chaplain at Coventry Hospital, had introduced two couples who had lost young sons the same night. They talked, cried out their sorrows, cared for one another, and found, after a year, that they survived better for sharing their awful bereavement. They asked Simon to help them organize a group of people who would help others by loving them back to life again. The Society of Compassionate Friends was begun.

We corresponded with Simon for over a year before he came to the United States to help start the first American branch of the Society of Compassionate Friends. From him we began to learn about the natural process of grief we had already been experiencing and about how those who have "been there" are able to help others to cope with the death of their loved one. Simon confirmed our feeling that there is no death so saddening as the death of your beloved child. This tragic blow takes away from every parent his or her raison d'être — because our children are our future. Everything becomes nothing. When parents lose a child, the normal cycle of their lives is upset radically. Their will to go on is destroyed; their future, their hopes and plans, and the meaningfulness of the family all are obscured; they are "as nothing."

The shock of child loss and the destruction of the entire parental reason for being is so traumatic an event that the community does not know how to face the problem, nor how to help the parents cope with their loss. When a child dies, the parents are usually surrounded by relatives and friends — at first — and are allowed to express their grief, at the funeral and during the mourning periods. But what happens after a few weeks or months? The anesthetic of the initial stunning shock wears off; and the relatives and friends, who came so quickly to help, have drifted back to their own concerns and to the demands of their own daily lives. The bereaved parents often find themselves alone, uncared for, depressed and feeling abandoned and unable to cope with the mass of painful problems of readjustment to life without their beloved child.

The Book of Job (19:13–14) describes the situation:

My brothers stand aloof from me, and my relations take care to avoid me. My kindred and friends have all gone away, and the guests in my house have forgotten me.

Modern society smothers the whole topic of death and bereavement in silence and embarrassment. Simon calls this the "conspiracy of silence." The reality of grief is denied, and there are few outlets for pent-up anxieties, tensions, guilt feelings, anger, loneliness, loss of faith, and hopelessness about the future.

These stresses frequently appear as physical symptoms: aches and pains, real illnesses, exhaustion, and loss of motivation. Drugs may bring passing relief, but the underlying anguish needs to be relieved by talking freely to an understanding and compassionate friend. Too often bereaved parents get little help from their ministers, priests, or rabbis, or from their doctors and their psychologists. Time after time, professionals are inadequate and ineffective in counseling bereaved parents and guiding them in their desperate need to find reasons to go on after the loss of a child — unless they too are bereaved parents.

The first key to caring for bereaved parents is other parents who themselves have lost children, who have felt what the newly bereaved are suffering. These are really the ones able to offer the understanding that permits parents to work out their griefs, to cry out their pain, to learn to live and love again.

Arnold and I were very impressed with the philosophy and the workings of the Society of Compassionate Friends. We wanted to help others to cope with what we had lived through and learned about, and realized that by doing so our burdens would become lighter. On October 12, 1972, with Simon's help, we started the first branch of the

Society of Compassionate Friends in the United States. A great deal of local publicity helped us bring together bereaved parents in the greater Miami–Fort Lauderdale area for monthly meetings. At these meetings, there was usually a guest speaker — a psychologist, a doctor, a minister or rabbi, or a case worker in a crisis intervention center. These talks generated many questions, much discussion, and free and open talk among the members. People could talk without fear of put-downs, rejection, listener boredom, criticism, indifference, insensitivity, or platitudes. They could discuss, they could cry, they could be angry, they could express their loss of religious faith, and they would be accepted by those who had felt the same things.

Question and answer periods revolved around a great variety of subjects, from medical and legal questions to personal questions, such as what to do with the child's pictures and toys and clothes; how to face changing the child's room. There are no consistent answers to these questions, but by letting the bereaved parent verbalize his or her questions freely and exchange ideas with those who have had the same questions before, answers do come and unpressured solutions evolve.

Through meetings, too, parents have made new connections and developed firm and lasting friendships.

The group broadened its scope to communicate with newly bereaved parents to disseminate information on death and bereavement in the media. The group also worked with professionals in the audience to help them better help bereaved parents to cope. The more Arnold and I worked with our local group, the more we saw how right was the philosophy of newly bereaved parents being helped by those who had already traveled the path. By listening to others speak of their grief, by sharing similar experiences and feelings, and by caring for each other, over time our wounds would lessen. We saw others coming back to life, as we were, by participating in this important work.

Since October of 1972, with the help of both local and national publicity and a huge correspondence with parents, clergy, doctors, nurses, social workers, funeral directors, psychologists, and family counselors across the country — all interested in the problems of death and bereavement — Arnold and I have helped start many additional branches of the Society of Compassionate Friends in the United States. Today, the Compassionate Friends is a national corporation with headquarters in Illinois. Made up of hundreds of chapters all across the country, it is one of the largest and most successful self-help groups in our time.

Arnold and I learned that there is no death so tragic or so sad as the death of one's child. Yet, we coped with this tragedy, first by trial and error and then by participating in the positive activity of helping others and ourselves through the pain. We have been a part of people loving people, sharing and caring for one another, making this most negative of life's experiences into something positive. Our reward has been in helping others to live and love themselves and love life again enough to go on despite what they have experienced. Through our experiences we learned that with love and caring there is no death. We, and all parents who participate in this experience, do so in loving memory of our beloved children.

Diana Gabrielle Shamres, this was for you.

Paula Shamres

After more than a year of chemotherapy and radiation treatments, Mark died of leukemia on December 24, 1975, at the age of thirteen.

Sharon and Ben Smith worked through the death of their only child by helping to launch the first Ronald McDonald House to be owned and operated by parents. This home away from home is open to families whose children are being treated for cancer or leukemia at nearby children's hospitals. Ben, chairman of the board of Children's Oncology Services of Illinois, is the head of the Science Department of Oak Lawn Community High School. Sharon has recently returned to teaching first graders how to read, something she calls "a very rewarding experience." "We have learned that the only way you can really find love is to give it away. Like a smile, it returns."

A TEENAGER DIES

Let Love Flower Again

Against incredible odds we reached our goal. We both finished the university with graduate degrees. Ben received his Ph.D. and I had my Master's degree after twelve years at the university and twelve years of marriage. In 1972 we believed we had a promising future. We had our formal education, new jobs and a beautiful ten-year-old son. Mark grew up being interested in nature. He loved to draw birds in their natural settings. He was a perfectionist. He excelled in mathematics. He was the joy of our lives.

Two years later Mark was at our side as we listened to Dr. Edward Baum of Children's Memorial Hospital in Chicago describe his illness. We were in a strange city, in an unfamiliar hospital, listening to words and learning about drugs we had never heard of before. Dr. Baum, a pediatric oncologist/hematologist, was telling us that our twelve-year-old son had cancer.

Every parent of a seriously ill child knows that a great deal of confusion follows diagnosis and treatment. Our family struggled each day for thirteen months to maintain some semblance of normal family life. On December 24, 1975, despite chemotherapy and radiation treatments, our son died.

We were devastated by the loss. As parents of an only child, we had lost our family and our future. I mourned for our child and the grandchildren that would never be. Ben and I had no reason for planning ahead. We had no real meaning in our lives — no purpose — no goals.

Each new day brought more loneliness and unbearable silence. Ben longed for the son who was always at his side trying out a new wrestling hold, romping on the floor. I ached to hold my child again.

During this time, I became preoccupied with my thoughts. I would stare endlessly into space, my mind wandering over every detail of Mark's illness. I had so many questions about his illness and treatment. Not getting answers, I became angry with the doctors and with God. I talked to very few people. Because most of our friends, neighbors, and acquaintances had children and a family, it became harder and harder to get myself out of the house.

About a year after Mark died, we learned about a parent-doctor nonprofit organization formed by Charles and Gay Marino, Dr. Edward Baum, and a group of parents who had children with cancer or leukemia. The Marinos recognized a desperate need for temporary housing for parents of seriously ill children who were being treated at Chicago's Children's Memorial Hospital. While their own daughter was gravely ill in the intensive care unit, they watched other parents sleeping on couches and chairs to be near their children. Parents from distances of a hundred miles or more were virtually living in hospital waiting rooms so they could be close to their sons and daughters.

From Dr. Baum, the Marinos learned about a Philadelphia facility for parents whose children came long distances for cancer treatment at Philadelphia's Children's Hospital. When the Marinos' daughter recovered, they flew to visit the Ronald McDonald House of Philadelphia. They talked to organizers of the House: Jim Murray, General Manager of the Philadelphia Eagles, and Dr. Audrey Evans of Children's Hospital. They learned that in 1973, Kim Hill, the seven-year-old daughter of Eagles' player Fred Hill, was being treated for leukemia by Dr. Evans. At that time, Fred Hill and Jim Murray went to Dr. Evans and asked her what they could do to help other children with leukemia. Together, the Eagles and the local McDonald restaurant owners and operators raised funds for a house where the families of the children could stay. They named this special home after Ronald, the fun-loving clown who represented hope to afflicted children and their parents. A child admitted to the hospital could relax knowing that Mom and Dad and even brothers and sisters were only a few blocks away at Ronald's house.

With renewed enthusiasm and a promise of help from Jim Murray, the Marinos came back to Chicago and began to search for suitable housing and financing for a Ronald McDonald House near Children's Memorial Hospital.

Ben and I were enthusiastic about the Ronald McDonald House project because we also had learned to sleep in chairs and couches while Mark was hospitalized. We hated to leave our son and drive forty miles home, so we often existed for days in the hospital without eating properly or having adequate sleep.

We met the Marino family and other parents who had children being treated for cancer at Children's Memorial

Hospital. We found that we shared a common bond with them. They understood what it was like to live with cancer and lose a child to this disease. They understood that along with the loss of our son, we felt useless. We no longer felt needed.

This group of parents put us to work on the Ronald McDonald House of Chicago. Although it was the second Ronald McDonald House, it was the first House of its kind to be initiated, owned, and operated by a group of parents. These parents and their doctors were not wealthy people, but they had unlimited energy and motivation to keep this beautiful three-story Victorian home filled to capacity and running smoothly. Can you think of a better way to get to know other parents in similar circumstances than by hanging pictures on the wall or deciding on the color of a rug together? Ben and I mopped floors, cleaned the kitchens, hung towel racks, and helped the other parents with the many details needed to keep an eighteen-bedroom house functioning. We became professional beggers as we helped solicit air conditioners, linens, dishes, mattresses, and furniture.

Using the talents he had acquired growing up on a large dairy farm, Ben took charge of the house maintenance. The parent who was in charge of house operations loved to comment that he had the only Ph.D. in charge of maintenance at a Ronald McDonald House. We felt useful there. Our work made a difference.

The newly formed nonprofit organization called Children's Oncology Services of Illinois, Inc., (COSI) opened the Ronald McDonald House on April 27, 1977. It was a home away from home for families whose children were being treated for cancer or leukemia at nearby Children's Memorial Hospital. A family could have a clean room, kitchens in which to cook their meals, and laundry facilities — all for $5.00 a night if they could afford it. If this expense was a burden, Children's Oncology Services assumed the costs. At the House, too, these families found others who were learning to live with cancer or another serious illness and could begin to share sorrow and hope.

Ben became president of COSI in the fall of 1978 and chairman of the board in 1979. Through the efforts of the parent group and the generosity of the entire Chicago metropolitan area, COSI burned the mortgage on the first anniversary of the opening of the House. The Association of Chicagoland McDonald Restaurant Owners and Operators had pledged $150,000 toward the project and exceeded their pledge as they held promotions on our behalf. Donations were made by school groups, organizations, and individuals; the project, which cost approximately $500,000, was a reality and it was paid in full.

From the beginning COSI received phone calls and requests from people who wanted to visit the Chicago House. Physicians and parent groups came from all over the United States, Canada, Australia, and other countries. A national COSI group was organized and an advisory committee was formed to help interested groups in other cities. By July 1, 1980, seventeen Ronald McDonald Houses were operating to provide temporary housing for families whose children were receiving treatment at the nearby children's hospitals.

During the summer of 1978, COSI expanded its program with a summer camp for children with cancer and leukemia. The first year over one hundred children from Illinois and Wisconsin attended our One Step at a Time Camp. For most of these children it was the first time they had been away from their families since diagnosis. It was also the first time their parents had a respite from the constant day-by-day care. Kids from seven through eighteen were able to continue their chemotherapy, receive blood counts, and be closely supervised since COSI took a complete medical team to camp. Dr. Baum, Dr. Harry Wilson, nurses, a medical technologist, and many parents volunteered their time so these children could swim, play ball, and enjoy arts and crafts like any other children going off to summer camp.

In 1979 and 1980, One Step at a Time was enlarged to accommodate 160 to 180 kids. A Campcrafter program, affectionately known as "tent city" was begun. It involved thirty teenagers camping in tents, carrying their own water, and assisting in the cooking and clean-up.

In July 1980 the teenagers traveled one hundred miles from the regular camp for a three-day expedition where they set up a new campsite, pitching their own tents. It was a memorable day when, under the guidance of a trained rock climbing instructor, the kids climbed a forty-foot rock face. Of the twenty-five youngsters physically able to attempt the climb, twenty-four succeeded in climbing to the top. It was a real boost to their self-image. Some of the counselors were so inspired by seeing them attempt the difficult climb that they had to try to make it themselves. The day after the rock climb, these same kids went on a twenty-mile canoe trip where they were able to use some of the skills they had learned in camp.

Perhaps our favorite experience was a five-day trip to Orlando, Florida, for 108 kids from nine cancer centers in the Chicago and Wisconsin area. Fifty-five parents, twelve COSI chaperones, and five medical people shared in the "American Dream Flite" in April 1980.

Every child under the age of eleven traveled with one parent. Children over ten were part of small groups of three or four, chaperoned by one COSI parent. All chaperones had been directly affected by cancer; seven of the twelve parent chaperones had lost a child to this disease. Our medical team was led by Dr. June Fusner of Milwaukee's Children's Hospital.

We visited Disney World, Sea World, and Circus World. The children escaped briefly into the world of Shamu, the killer whale, of circus clowns, and the magic of the wonderful world of Disney. Ben took more trips on Space Mountain than he can remember as he and Dr. Jim Nachman accompanied the excited kids. There were some memorable moments. Ben shared one: "As we began to take off on the Florida Hurricane in Circus World, I watched three girls in the seat ahead of me take off their wigs as a precaution for the upcoming thrills, shocking the ride operator as he stared at bare heads." The girls had developed a closeness that provided them the security to expose their loss of hair, one of the most traumatic experiences that young girls with cancer can face.

At the hotel, I watched the kids scream with laughter as they jumped into the pool with Dr. Nachman. Fourteen of our kids were leg amputees and were seemingly at ease in swimming suits by the pool.

As beneficial as the trip itself was, even more valuable was the chance for the parents and children to share time with other parents and children who had similar problems. At curfew time one night my girls were still sitting around the pool just talking. I had to send them back to their rooms, but I hated to ask them to leave each other.

During camp and the Florida trip we discovered the importance of providing peer group experiences for these kids with cancer. Too often, they are isolated in their communities; they may not even attend school because teachers, parents, and the kids themselves think they are not capable of regular activities. We know this is not so — and our kids are proving it. COSI has established a Boy Scout Explorer Post for boys and girls with cancer. We've planned monthly excursions for kids: cross-country skiing, canoeing, boating, and camping. We're even preparing for an eleven-day backpacking trip into the mountains!

Friends and family members have asked Ben and me about our involvement with other children who have cancer. They fear it may become too much for us to be reminded of the past. I can't deny that it hurts to see a youngster who is afflicted with cancer. But we share with him or her and the family an understanding of the fears, concerns, and special needs in dealing with the disease.

We care. Through our energies, we can attempt to make the child's life and that of the family more comfortable and more meaningful, and our involvement makes our own lives more meaningful as well.

We have found that being around young people whether they are ill or healthy has given us the chance to experience the renewal and potential of youth. The young are a reminder that life does go on. We have been richly blessed with the love of our son, our family, and friends. We have learned that the only way you can really find love is to give it away. Like a smile, it returns.

Sharon and Ben Smith

David, an army medic, was shot by a sniper in Germany on March 14, 1945.

David's mother, Betty Bryce, of Lake Orion, Michigan, is the national president of the American Gold Star Mothers. Founded in 1928, Gold Star Mothers is composed of women whose children were killed on active duty or died subsequently as a result of wounds. There are currently 8000 members in chapters around the country.

Mrs. Bryce has worked as a beautician, rental agent, and practical nurse in a hospital setting.

WHEN A SON IS KILLED IN WAR

Use Grief Constructively

I am a Gold Star Mother. I lost an eighteen-year-old son in World War II, in Germany. This is the story of how I have lived through the thirty-five years following his death.

June 12, 1944. David had just graduated from high school. He was valedictorian of his class and had a college scholarship. He came in that day and said, "I have signed up for immediate induction." I looked at him and somehow I knew this was the beginning of something that would touch *all* our lives. He was home once for ten days. Little did I know that those ten days would have to last me for the rest of my life.

December 7, 1944. When we put him on the bus, my heart was broken. I told my husband, "This is it. We will never see him again." Somehow I knew. Then began the days of watching for the mailman. Each time a letter came it was a day of relief. Sometimes I would write two or three letters a day. This helped to ease my worry.

March 29, 1945. No letters for two weeks. One night I was awakened from sleep. I sat up and said, "You killed my son." I knew something had happened. That day I was very restless. There was a light rain falling, but I had to get out of the house. I was raking leaves when a car drove up in front of my next-door neighbor's house. The man looked at me, then went to her door. She had just moved in a week before and I was not yet acquainted with her. They both came up to me and the gentleman said, "I have bad news for you." There it was, the telegram that said, REGRET TO INFORM YOU THAT YOUR SON WAS KILLED IN ACTION. How do you explain how you feel when your world has crashed with eleven little words?

No one but another Gold Star Mother can understand what those words meant. I thought of the words in the Bible: "Greater love hath no man than that he lay down his life for a friend." I pondered them many times in the days and months that followed. One day, I was looking out the window at some small children playing. I said to myself, "They can play without fear because boys like David were willing to give their lives if necessary." It was some comfort.

After the telegram, not much news followed. I wanted so much to know what happened. Was he alone when he died? Did he suffer long? Where did they bury him? I prayed every day for more information. Then the boxes of food — thirteen of them we had sent — and over a hundred letters, were returned marked "deceased." I cried many tears and I wrote to everyone whose name appeared in the letters. One day I received a letter in answer to one of them. It was from a chaplain. "David," he wrote, "was not alone. Not even a sparrow falls that God does not know about."

At times like this, everyone begins to question the will of God. All of us, at some point in our lives, ask ourselves:

"Why did God let this happen to me? Am I being punished?" People have said, piously, "We must accept it. It's God's will." I do not believe this. His will for our lives is good. I do not believe it was His will for my son to be cut down at the age of eighteen.

This tragedy did change a fear I had. I was always afraid of death. Since David has gone, that has passed. I read somewhere, "If death is only a sleep, then how sweet sleep is. If one lives after death then that also is good." I believe prayers are answered.

After several months when I so desperately wanted to hear from someone who had seen David or spoken to him, a letter came from the government with a letter enclosed from a twelve-year-old Belgian girl. She had spoken to him when his outfit was passing through her country. She had visited the cemetery near where she lived in Liège and saw his name on a cross. She wrote to me. What a lift that was! My prayer had been answered. We corresponded for ten years. This was what I needed. I wanted to be able to place a flower and offer a prayer at his grave. This is what she did for me. I received many pictures showing her placing flowers and offering a prayer. These things were such a comfort to me, to know that someone cared. When I asked her if there was anything I could do for her, she said, "No, we owe our lives to boys like David." She called me her American Mom. She sent me word when the cemetery was closed and arrangements were being made to send the body home.

As I sit and write these things, so many memories return. The day two military men came and presented David's medals to us. Here in my hand was placed a Purple Heart and the Silver Star for service beyond the call of duty. My thoughts traveled back to when he was in high school and running track. When he was ready to leave for an event I would always say, "Bring me back a ribbon."

And there I sat holding the last of his awards. He did his best to the last. I can only weep for what might have been.

I am very depressed at different times of the year — especially holidays. On December 7, we put David on the bus. It was the last time we saw him. Christmas Day at 10:00 A.M. he called me from New York. He was being shipped out. On Easter weekend, we received the notice of his death and he arrived home for reburial the day before Armistice Day.

The first year was a very hard one to get through. I would read and re-read his letters trying to find some comfort in them. I would go through those letters several times a week until one day I came to grips with myself. I took stock of things. I had a husband. I had two other children who were depending on me. So I took a piece of luggage and put all the mementos in it. I felt like I had closed a book on that part of my life. I must live for the future. There must be something I could do to help others.

I am sure there are many Gold Star Mothers who could write a similar story. At first, I turned against the German people. Then the thought came to me that their hearts were also broken when their children were killed. I learned to be tolerant and to forgive. War is caused by human selfishness, greed, and wickedness. It is the family who suffers.

Looking back over the years, I know that the thing that has helped me most is my association with other Gold Star Mothers. It was a Gold Star Mother forming a chapter in our town, who came to me in my darkest hour. She said, "Come join us." They understood me. It is hard to talk to someone who was untouched by a war. They change the subject. We Gold Star Mothers can talk to each other. A few tears are shed. This is good. We know the pain of war. There is much love for each other. The work that is done for the boys in our veteran's hospitals and for their mothers is very rewarding. It is good to give of ourselves. When our son was returned for reburial, it was the Gold Star Mothers who were there. They helped and understood.

After David's death, I went into nursing. It was another outlet for me — ministering to the wants of the ill and holding their hands when the end was near. The hurt is still with me. Many nights I still cry myself to sleep. I am trying to live so that when it is my time to die, then, I shall meet my son. He will reach out to me and say, "Hello, Mother." All my questions will be answered. God was good to me. I have another son and a very devoted daughter. The peace of mind I have sought is now with me. God is good.

Betty Bryce

WHAT HELPED
When a Husband or Wife Dies

When a spouse dies, you lose your present.

Sheila was killed in an automobile accident in Colorado in August 1970. Her husband, Peter Stringham, is a physician in a neighborhood health center. There has been much research about the problems of the wife whose husband has died. Little has been understood about the special emotional and practical problems of the millions of widowers.

They too have their difficulties coping with grief and loneliness in a couple-oriented society. There are the complexities of separating themselves from their deceased wives and reintegrating themselves into a singles' world that has changed radically since they were married. If they are parents, they may wonder how they will manage the many situations involving the children that their wives handled before. What about remarriage — its problems and possibilities? Contrary to popular "wisdom," the widower is not always carefree, debonair, and jaunty.

Two years after his wife's tragic death, Dr. Peter Stringham met Jean. "I could truly know my first marriage was good, but that it was over." They are now happily married.

A FATAL ACCIDENT

Being in Pain Is Normal

At the age of twenty-seven my life was as complete as I could imagine. Sheila and I were happily married, living on an Indian reservation in New Mexico, where I loved working as a doctor while avoiding the Vietnam war. Our one-and-a-half-year-old daughter, Zoe, was talking well and adjusting nicely to her brother, Guy, a newborn who had just been placed with us for adoption. As a family, we were content and complete.

I had been up late at night with patients and had driven the one hundred miles to Colorado to see patients all day in another clinic. I was tired and glad when Sheila offered to drive the four of us back home. I woke up as our van fell off the road onto a soft shoulder, started down a small hill, flipped over, and crunched to a violent halt. Both children were crying; Sheila's door was open — her seat belt unused — and it was very quiet. On the usually deserted road a group of archeology students saw the accident and stopped. Two took Zoe and Guy and a third helped me look for Sheila. I ran through the grass calling for her, puzzled, but not terribly afraid. Everything was quiet.

After what seemed like an endless time of increasing panic (perhaps only a few minutes), the student found her yards away from the van. Agonal breathing, twitching, and, to my horror, dilated pupils . . . the look of death. I tried to breathe for her, but she kept filling up with blood. We tried for a long time. A state patrol car stopped, and another passerby said, "There were four in this van; this one is dead." I knew he was right. The students drove us the thirty miles to the nearest town. Zoe had only a minor scrape; Guy was very fussy and needed to be checked; and I needed stitches on my bottom lip.

On the way to the hospital, my emotions went on a roller coaster. One minute I would be weeping, seeing the accident and Sheila dying, and the next minute I would feel almost normal. I would think, "This is such a surprise. Do you believe it? I don't. A surprise, like a May snowstorm that covers the leafed-out trees, breaks branches, and disrupts everything. I feel like this is a May snowstorm — odd, not catastrophic. That's probably wrong, but it's the best I can do." One moment I wanted to make small talk, and the next I felt like a cartoon character who had been smashed in the head with a club.

By the time we reached the emergency room, I felt no need for small talk. I was totally disorganized, my emotions washing over me in waves. I acted like a robot, but felt irritation, indecision, helplessness, and a terrible tiredness. I needed a familiar face, but the people closest to me were all away on vacation. I asked the staff to call Betty, a public health nurse whom I didn't know too well, but I thought she could be of help because her husband had died that year. She came over to the emergency room immediately. She said nothing, but held me and cried with me. After Guy was admitted to the hospital, she took Zoe and me home.

For the next day and a half, Betty helped me with my disorganization and confusion. I knew enough to call New Mexico and arrange for a doctor to cover my clinic, but I thought that I shouldn't bother Sheila's parents that night with such bad news. Betty assured me they would want to know right away. She helped me make a list of people to telephone and took care of Zoe while I made each exhausting call.

In her calm and unobtrusive way, Betty helped me review my options for the children. She pointed out that I could care for Zoe well in New Mexico with a live-in housekeeper. After discussing choices about Guy, I concluded that as a single parent I probably had lost my claim on him and that he really needed a mother. Betty gently agreed that this was a good decision, and I added the adoption worker to my list. The next day I said a sad good-bye to Guy before he left.

The burial plans confused and exhausted me. Sheila and I had never talked about our deaths. I thought cremation in Colorado would be the easiest and least expensive plan. Her parents wanted her body flown back to New York for a burial. Betty wisely pushed me toward a burial in New York, saying it would mean a great deal to Sheila's family. She reminded me of my appointment with the undertaker. In the two days that I was with Betty, she gave me many suggestions about what had been helpful when her husband died.

When I got home, I felt "normal," but the exhausted, drained feeling persisted and my tolerance for other people's idiosyncracies was gone. A very inquisitive and eccentric neighbor, whom I had easily tolerated before Sheila's death, greeted me as soon as I returned and asked excitedly about the details of the accident. I wanted to scream. I cut the conversation very short and shook with sobs after she left.

Later that night, my mother arrived tense and upset. I felt I couldn't help her deal with her emotions. I was irritable and furious. As she tried to say the right thing, the supportive thing, I thought, "Emily Post has no rules for this one." She busied herself with Zoe and packed for her. When she asked if she could pack for me, I snapped back that I could pack for myself. The next day I left the house in rubber wading boots; I forgot my shoes and needed to buy a pair before our plane left. I felt stupid, ungrateful, and childish, but still annoyed. My mother tolerated my fury with sad wonder.

In New York I was frazzled and afraid, but determined that I would handle anything. I tried to anticipate each event and cried alone until I could face it. I walked into the viewing room and did not fall apart, cry, or scream. I looked for friends, checked out the room, and felt in control. But I had not anticipated the heart-shaped wreath with "To Mommy from Zoe and Guy" on it; tears and sobs choked me. I was an odd sight — calm and smiling one moment, sobbing violently the next. The visiting hours and funeral continued in the same way. I steeled myself for whatever public event came next and got through it, crying only a few times an hour. Sometimes I'd think, "This is not real; it is just a surprise. This is odd, not catastrophic." Then I'd be a weeping, wounded child, a weak husband who couldn't provide a stable family for his children and a bad doctor who couldn't save his own wife from dying. I thought people would think, "He must be a completely disgusting human being and we ought to take the last child away from him quickly before something happens to her." I mostly cried alone.

After the funeral, at my in-laws' frantic household, Zoe retreated to the quiet arms of eighty-one-year-old Uncle Jack. After his first wife had died in the 1917 influenza epidemic, he had raised four small children before marrying Sheila's Aunt Dot. He seemed to be watching me to see whether I was all right. He was recovering from a stroke and his only words were, "I'm so sorry, Doc. I'm so sorry." I thought, "He knows, and he doesn't consider me disgusting." I also saw his deep sorrow, and I knew that the "this is a surprise — so odd" feeling was an illusion and that things were going to get a lot worse. But Uncle Jack had made it and so would I.

My brother David offered to drive Zoe and me back to New Mexico. We stopped at my parents' house, and although they couldn't afford it, they gave me money to pay off the loan on the wrecked van. We visited friends, and I remember telling funny stories and making people laugh and almost feeling that nothing had happened. But I noticed my zest for life was gone. A midnight swim in a lake after a wood-fired sauna was exhilarating, but somehow not that exhilarating. David wanted to drive after some hot air balloonists, but I had no interest.

Zoe ran through a friend's house calling, "Mommy, Mommy." I choked back a sob and said, "She's dead, but I'm here." I was afraid for her. As we rode along the next day, I held Zoe and began to write a lullaby. I felt that if I could sing this song without crying, I would have faced reality enough so that I could meet her needs and keep her life all right. I kept saying to myself, "I will not let your mother's death hurt you. I will make up for this loss."

> Go to sleep my baby boo.
> Your mother would be proud of you.
> You're talking so, and you're not two,
> But she's lying in the graveyard.

> Go to sleep my honey bun.
> You had a brother; now he's gone.
> You lost a playmate, I . . . my son and
> Your mommy in the graveyard.

> Go to sleep my little pet.
> Your mommy, she would cry I'll bet
> For all the things that you'll not get 'cause
> She's lying in the graveyard.

I thought I'd never forget the other three verses, for I've sung them thousands of times, but I have.

The evening after I had written most of the lullaby I went to bed and got the shakes. I couldn't cry in front of David. He was five years younger, and I was not over the older brother role yet. I lay in bed with chattering teeth and twitching muscles, unable to stop. Embarrassed and ashamed for being so weak, I finally said, "I can't stop shaking." David wasn't embarrassed. He held me until the shaking stopped and I fell asleep.

The first week back home, with help from the townspeople, I hired Anna, an Apache grandmother, who had known and liked Sheila. With Anna settled as a live-in housekeeper, I felt like a whirlwind of energy. Usually I could get pleasure from working on artistic projects, but this week nothing seemed to satisfy me. Neither recording the lullaby nor making a movie helped. Although I filled the movie with the most bizarre images I could conceive — burning baby carriages, a watermelon filled with feath-

84

ers, and a blood throwing monster — the movie felt far less bizarre than my life.

One night I went for a walk alone. My brother was leaving, and I was uncertain about how supportive my local friends would be. "Look Sheila," I wept, speaking to her for the first time since she died, "I've done everything right. Zoe's all right. Guy will be all right. I'll be all right. I'm really doing well. I've been so strong . . . if I could just talk to you." And suddenly I felt she could come back. How could I have been so blind? She could come back! I beat on the side of the road very quietly, so that no one would know I was crazy. I screamed, "Come back, come back! You must come back! I beg you, please come back." She had been dead a month.

Over the next months my feelings about Sheila changed. The feeling that she probably would return at the end of one month was gradually modified so that I felt she could return, but only if she wanted to. I concluded she didn't want to return because she hated us. But I knew she loved the children, so she must have hated me.

Later I felt that although she could not return, she had deliberately died because she hated me. Only after she had been dead six months, did I believe that she had not hated me, had not chosen to die, and could not return.

My many friends in New Mexico and elsewhere helped me the most over those months, but my quicksilver changes of emotions confused them, and a few of them disappointed me. Some people gave me the unspoken message, "You chose to come back here; don't expect me to solve your problems." One friend left the room whenever I talked about Sheila's death. Most friends were helpful and told me their own stories about grieving which I desperately wanted to hear. I needed to know what other people had done and felt like and that I was normal. One friend told me that his wish to telephone his mother for months after she died had made him think that he was crazy.

Peg, the head nurse at the clinic, became an especially important person. A man whom she loved had died of an illness several years before, and despite my fear that no one could understand, Peg really did. She told me she could not stop my pain, but that she would listen to me. Several times a week, after Zoe was asleep, I would go to her house to have a drink and know I was not alone. She listened to me for months, kept me from being too rude or obnoxious to other people, and used her sense of humor to help me sort out what was real from what I was misperceiving. I cried every day for five months and often with Peg.

Besides talking to Peg and other friends, I tried to express and understand my feelings through painting pictures. I had painted since medical school. I'd put exuberant designs on the van. For four months I painted pictures of distorted, beaten, twisted men. I saw a psychotherapist in New York at Christmas and told him that I worried my anger would never cease. Would I end my days an infuriated and infuriating man? He told me two things: First, my anger would change to sadness when I felt Sheila had lost more than I, and second, part of Sheila might live if her best qualities were alive in me.

I returned to New Mexico and abandoned the tortured men to paint pictures of Sheila in an effort to feel sorry for her. I was not at all sorry for her, just angry. She had escaped, leaving us to suffer and adjust. I painted and stared, and painted again. Slowly, after nearly three identical pictures I began to see that she had lost all of us and her life. Sheila lost the most. For the first time I could cry for her sake. This was six months after she died.

The next month I hit bottom. I felt nothing. I could sing the death lullaby and not cry or feel sorry for myself.

I saw my life without anger at Sheila, God, myself, or anyone. My life was bleak and empty. I painted a picture of myself and felt nothing. I did not cry that day, but I hated it.

Idly over the next month, I began to make some Indian-looking wall hangings out of feathers, bones, medallions, roots, and fur. The robes were shaman's costumes that a magician would use to solve problems — to drive out despair. While making the second robe, I knew something was missing. I'd summoned up all the magic a shaman could muster — the sea, the land, the air, drugs, Christianity, and magic — but something was missing. In a flash I realized the missing element was a sense of joy — Sheila's sense of joy. I made and added a Mardi Gras mask and, after that, slowly began to add a sense of joy to my life again. I enjoyed Zoe a lot more and was less depressed when I spent time with her. I liked my work better, spoke to a Rotary Club about drugs, and talked on a Colorado radio station as part of a panel. My depression was lifting.

But setbacks surprised me. On Mother's Day, which Sheila and I had never celebrated, I was terribly and unexpectedly depressed.

Dating and sex could have been a problem, but a friend's words the week after Sheila died were helpful. She said that when her first husband suddenly deserted her, she regressed sexually to early teenage years and very slowly worked up from there, not resuming sexual relations for a year later. This was true for me. When some friends tried to introduce me to an eligible woman nine months after the accident, I felt insulted. "How could they possibly think she could be acceptable compared to Sheila?" Looking back, she was acceptable, but that evening I was curt and unfriendly and left them confused and angry. They forgave me, but only after many months.

One year after the accident, I said good-bye to my New Mexico friends, sent a letter to Guy who had been adopted, and moved to Boston. With a nine-to-five job as a neighborhood health center physician and a day care center for Zoe, now two and a half, I felt ready to begin a new relationship with a woman. After much painful dating and several relationships, I met Jean. When I sensed we might have a future together, I began to feel love for Jean. I remembered, "I used to feel like this all the time." I could truly know my first marriage was good, but that it was over. Two years after Sheila's death, I married Jean, who has loved me, Zoe, our new son, Eddie, and Sheila's family well over the last eight years.

My life is very precious to me. I love Jean, my children, my friends, my work, and my hobbies. I love being alive. Sheila *did* lose the most by dying and that still makes me sad.

Peter Stringham

In 1960, Dr. George Berg died, leaving a young family — a wife and three children, aged six, four, and one.

A year and a half later, his wife, Hélène, married Joseph Narot, an eminent clergyman. After eighteen years, Joseph took his own life.

Hélène Narot, a social worker, contrasts the avenues of help from the perspective of two very different kinds of death.

There are ten million American widows. Very few are merry. On the contrary, all too many emerge from the numbness of initial grief to a rude succession of shocks and disillusionments. Learning to be single again takes time and pain. A widow is often treated as a helpless invalid one day and as a social outcast the next; as a martyr for a month and a fifth wheel thereafter. It takes great effort to summon all of the resources — emotional, intellectual, and psychological — to face the new challenges of her altered life.

Widows are often relieved to hear what Helen Hayes, the distinguished actress, had to say about her adjustment to widowhood. She admitted candidly, "For two years I was just as crazy as can be and still be at large. It was total confusion. How did I come out of it? I don't know, because I didn't know I was in it when I was in it."

SURVIVING THE DEATHS OF TWO HUSBANDS

Find Strength within Yourself

In a span of twenty years I have suffered two great losses, both of my husbands have died. The feelings that I felt, the bereavement I experienced at these two different stages of my life, were so diverse that it is difficult to see them as the same process. Yet there are similarities as well as the obvious differences in bereavement as a young woman and a middle-aged one.

George was thirty-five and I was thirty when we learned that he had Hodgkin's disease. It had developed beyond the stage for successful treatment. He was doomed to die. How could this happen to George, a brilliant, creative, and caring physician just beginning his practice; a loving, warm, humorous, and involved father and husband? How could this happen to our children, aged six, four, and one, and to me, who depended on him for so much? We learned for the first time, but certainly not the last, that life is not fair.

During George's illness my source of strength came from him. He spent his days training me to be alone. He taught me practical skills — how to invest money, how to plan the children's education, how to find and use expert advice when I needed it. But more important, he grieved with me. Together we laughed and cried and cursed our fate; we loved and played and talked and talked. We asked ourselves if we were "bad" people that we should be so punished. George began to believe in the immortality of souls — a new concept for him. Together we planned to possibly meet again at another time and place. Whenever he felt strong enough, we would pile the kids into the car and go off for an adventure — a ride in the Goodyear blimp, or a visit to the creatures in the Everglades. George was always honest, open, supportive, and *living* his experience of dying. I was the same, so as not to miss one precious moment of sharing on his level.

When George died nine months after the diagnosis, my immediate feeling was relief. We had done our grieving, I thought, and the pain was over. Now it was time to get back to the world of the living. A month after the funeral, I traveled to New York City to spend a week exploring my new life. I bought new clothes, saw some Broadway shows, refurnished the bedroom where he had lain suffering, and tried desperately and somewhat successfully to "come back" to the world. But the pain was not gone. Returning home to face the world of loneliness was the real coming back. It was then that I found the source of strength in my bereavement — my children. They needed constant, daily attention and love. Whatever my feelings or needs, they needed to be fed, driven to school and lessons, played with, bathed, nurtured, and grieved with. Their needs to deal with losing George became my need to share this with them. Hardly ever did I have time for the indulgence of self-pity, though I longed to lapse into it.

In retrospect it is clear to me that as a thirty-one-year-old mother of three young children, and as the wife of a dying man and later his widow, I got the strength to function daily from outside myself. It came first from my dying husband and later from the needs of my children.

A year and a half after George's death I remarried. Joe was considerably older than I and had already reared his own children. Valiantly he set about being a father to my three. "Daddy George" was always in the picture, spoken about lovingly by the children and me. It was a problem for Joe — being a fill-in for George. Joe was brilliant and creative in different ways. He was a community leader, teacher, orator, and writer. As a father he was eager to help the children, both with their schoolwork and their understanding of life. But he had problems that ran deep into his psyche, and these were eventually to cause our marriage to end. During the sixteen years that we were together, Joe helped to rear my children and was an inspiration to us all. The children, now grown, echo his perfectly spoken grammar and good syntax. They knew well that he would never allow a paper to be turned in to a teacher unless the language, spelling, and punctuation were perfect!

Two years after our marriage ended, Joe's life ended tragically with a suicide. Life had not provided what he wanted and needed when he decided to go out on his own. Now he was tired and decided to take control by taking his life.

How does one deal with the suicide of a loved one? What do grown children, aged twenty-six, twenty-four, and twenty-one, feel about losing a second father? What do we do with the anger and resentment that we feel along with the sorrow and sadness? In the ten years before Joe's suicide I had gone back to school and earned a Master's degree in clinical social work. My training, and some personal psychotherapy, had led me to a new understanding of myself. Now I was ready to find strength within myself to face this shocking new loss and the subsequent bereavement. No longer was it the children or any others who forced me to be a functioning person each day. It was I, myself. My own inner strength helped me carry on. The experiences of the past, recovering a large measure of my old self after George's death, gave me the assurance and the confidence that I could and would do it again. Knowing that I had been through so much, including divorce and a new career, helped me to discover what strength I possessed, and to know that I could use this strength however I chose.

Although I never found the answers to those questions I asked about suicide and loss, the answers became unimportant as the confidence in myself grew. I felt anger and resentment, but they did not overwhelm me. Life prevailed, after all. The children have grown into responsible independent adults, contributors to society. They may never know their true feelings nor, perhaps, will I. They are unusually close for siblings, sharing much of their lives with each other. Perhaps that is their source of strength.

There are new losses every day. New romantic involvements that end sadly, professional disappointments, financial investments that may not do well. Sometimes I have immense confidence that I can cope with them all, using my past experiences as models. Other times, the loneliness takes over and even feelings of despair. Friends lend their support and love, family remains very important, but my own growth through life experiences seems to be the most reliable and constant source of strength.

Hélène Narot

A person kills herself. Life is over. For the family, the tragedy is just beginning. Death by suicide brings the greatest of all affronts to those who remain. Those left behind experience not only the pain of separation but aggravated feelings of shame and self-blame. The act of self-destruction raises the inevitable questions "Why?" and "What could I have done to prevent it?" The person who ends a life leaves a perpetual psychological skeleton in the survivors' closet. In the words of Albert Camus, "There is but one truly philosophical problem and that is suicide."

Dr. Robert M. Meyer is a practicing pediatrician.

WHEN A SPOUSE TAKES HER LIFE

Turn to a Faith Beyond

My wife chose to end her own life, after one year of severe depression; a year marked by three lengthy hospitalizations, six therapists, and eight suicide gestures, before her successful suicide. That year was one of excruciating pain and horror for both of us. After the shock had begun to subside, after the endless (but much needed) calls and visits from friends and family, I found myself asking, not without a certain amount of guilt, "Why do I feel better already? Shouldn't I still be more grief stricken?" Slowly but surely, the answers to those questions have become clearer.

Most important, I think, is that, for me, my wife did not die when she jumped from the bridge. The beauty, the vibrant laugh, the dynamism — all that I had loved about her — had died long before. She was a talented writer — who not so coincidentally had written about suicide in the year preceding her illness — but she found it an overwhelming task even to sign a check in the months following her breakdown. The finality of her suicide was, and continues to be, a devastating reality, but I had been suffering a deep loss prior to her physical death. To witness her emotional and spiritual disintegration was, in many ways, much worse.

For one year, I went to work never knowing what I'd find upon my return. Trying to sleep at night, I often fantasized about the outcome of this nightmare. And when my wife did not respond to therapy and remained deeply depressed, when the days became weeks and the weeks months, the terrible realization that she might one day succeed in a suicide attempt recurred with increasing frequency and clarity. Such thoughts only served to heighten my fears, but they continued. One day, seven weeks before her death, I told a friend exactly where and how she would do it, as if it had come to me in a vision. To my horror, it happened just that way.

Many survivors suffer pangs of guilt following the death of a loved one. "If only I'd done this" can become a reverberating theme. When my wife became ill, I began weekly psychotherapy. I would recommend it to anyone in a similar situation. It took the better part of that year to understand that what was happening was not only not my fault, but also was not in any way within my control. When my wife chose to end her life, the decision had been hers and hers alone, for reasons that were hers and hers alone. This realization has helped. The sadness is difficult enough; compounding the pain with guilt serves no constructive purpose.

Prior to this time, I had been spared any great tragedies in my life. And I had regarded religion in the time of crisis as just another prescription for crutches. I surprised myself at just how comfortably I used those crutches. Surrounded by other worshipers at a service, reciting traditional prayers, or singing in unison, it was comforting to find that when my faith was running low, I could turn to another Faith which had stood the test of thousands of years. If that Faith and the people who trusted in it had survived, then so would I.

In the midst of my adversity, I noticed a tendency to retreat, not to bother anyone else with my misfortune. What a mistake! The love and support of family and friends, in letters, phone calls, visits, and invitations, were so gratifying and so enriching as to defy description. This caring continues to stand out in my mind as a bright spot in an otherwise bleak scenario. Reach out! Martyrdom is not a necessary part of the mourning process.

I have made a valuable *new* friend as well — time. The sadness can seem interminable, the pain relentless, but it does pass. The tears still come, unexpectedly, but with less intensity and less frequency. At first, the sudden waves of sadness knocked me down, but I have learned to stand up to them — all because of time. It seems too trite to mention, but too important to leave out.

The only script is that there is no script. Everyone copes in his or her own way. There is no prescribed method to mourning — general stages, perhaps, but within those stages there is tremendous variability. It took a while to realize that I needed to do what I felt was right at the time — that going to a film or a party might not be premature, or that staying in bed one morning was not necessarily an escape.

Certainly, I look daily for more answers, and can sometimes lose sight of my comforting insights when the grief becomes particularly acute. But more important than any intellectual or emotional coping mechanism is the knowledge that I have survived a terrible loss with some scars — but life goes on and I will survive.

Robert M. Meyer

WHAT HELPED
When a Parent Dies

When a parent dies, you lose your past.

In Pittsburgh, in 1961, Bea Decker founded an international organization for widows, They Help One Another Spiritually (THEOS).

On June 21, 1978, Bea Decker died in Pennsylvania. Her daughter, Roberta (Robbie), had from childhood been her mother's traveling companion and as she grew up conducted workshops from the viewpoint of a child's grief process. "Because I had grown up in THEOS and because I had three months to anticipate my mother's death, I should have been intellectually and emotionally prepared . . . But I wasn't."

The goal of THEOS is spiritual enrichment with educational programs for the widowed and their families. "Happiness is finding spiritual strength to meet the problems of life. God promises a Peace that passeth understanding. Seek your happiness in Him. Your sorrow will turn into joy!"

A DAUGHTER'S RESPONSE TO HER MOTHER'S DEATH

Write Down Your Feelings

I was twenty-two years old when my mother died. But I was no stranger to death. My father died when I was five. My mother turned her personal tragedy into an organization to help other young widows. Her simple effort which began in our church is now an international organization called They Help Each Other Spiritually (THEOS).

My first exposure to THEOS was as a child in the nursery provided during the monthly chapter meetings. Since none of my school friends came from single-parent families, THEOS offered the security of knowing that I wasn't the only child without a father. It was also a sanctuary where I was sure no one would ask: "Where does your daddy work?"

As I grew older and realized the benefit of my exposure to other children in similar circumstances, I thought of the need to expand our services to children. I began to travel with my mother to weekend retreats that THEOS sponsored across the United States and Canada. I led workshops for the parents, affording them insights into their children's feelings. This effort expanded to include their children. I helped to draw youngsters into discussions of what it is like to experience the death of a parent.

I continued to work with THEOS in college, where I majored in psychology. My senior year seemed to drag on forever as plans were made in preparation for my joining the THEOS staff as a full-time person.

Suddenly my whole world came to an abrupt stop. It was just three weeks before my graduation when I learned that my mother had an inoperable, swiftly growing cancer developing throughout her body.

From my readings, I had learned that a child who has lost one parent may have an increased fear that the remaining parent will die also. I had considered my mother's death. But I felt secure that she would *never* die. After all she was all I had. I needed her all the more. And I would look at all the people she had helped. I thought that surely nothing could happen that would interrupt a life that was giving so much to others.

But there it was. A diagnosis that offered little hope of life beyond three months. Three months! They might as well have said an hour. That was precious little time. I was determined to spend every minute with her. I didn't want to go back to school. Finishing meant nothing to me without my mother. All my dreams for the future had crumbled into uncertainties and fears.

I forced myself to go back to classes and was present for my graduation ceremonies even though my mother was too sick to attend.

For two months after graduation, I made my mother my entire life. Hardly a moment went by that I wasn't near her.

Then she was gone!

The days seemed endless. Nothing held any meaning. I knew that my mother would want me to go on and discover fulfillment for myself. I tried to embrace the principles of surviving that her life had personified.

Outwardly I kept up the appearance of functioning. I dressed nicely, had my hair restyled, and even did some major redecorating to make me accept "our" home as now "my" home. When I went through her personal belongings, I found a letter that my mother had written to a friend shortly after her own mother's death. She wrote,

I'm missing my Mom very much now as the holidays approach. But when I get the blues, I think of HER and not ME and right away I'm convinced she is where she deserves to be and would want to be. When you love someone very much, you always consider their wishes over yours and I know Mom would have wanted to go quickly rather than linger with cancer.

This letter created a lot of confusion and guilt. I wanted to be as accepting as Mom had been. But I wasn't. Of course I didn't want her to linger with cancer. But why did she have to get it in the first place? Why were we robbed of the future that we had dreamed of together? Why was I left alone? I was frightened. I was angry at God, and I'd lost the emotional support I used to receive from my mother.

I knew there were a lot of people watching me. I felt I had to express some grief or people would question the intensity of the love I had shared with my mother. So I'd tell them that I wasn't eating — often for days at a time — and that if they wanted to do something for me, I'd sure appreciate a meal.

At the same time, I felt that everyone wanted to know if I had absorbed all that Mom had taught. I couldn't express my deep feelings of loss, constant pain, or anger. I couldn't talk to my friends, I needed to hide behind a mask. I couldn't talk to my sisters. They were hurting so badly from their own grief that I didn't want to inflict additional pain and worry. I tried counseling. I was even able to fool the counselor with my mask.

I knew I had to find some outlet, especially when I began having dreams that left me waking in tears — dreams that wouldn't let me deny my real feelings.

That's when I began my writing. At first I had no special notebook; just wrote on whatever paper was available. I allotted no special time for writing, nor did I write every day. My style was not philosophical or poetic. I simply would write down my gut feelings as though I were talking to a very special friend.

It was about three months after Mom's death that I understood the need to be more precise. I was taking a continuing education course in journal writing. At my professor's suggestion, I bought a special notebook exclusively for these reflections. I set aside time each night before going to bed to record the day's activities. The initial objective of my journal was to record my stages of grief. Moments that I couldn't share with anyone, times that I didn't want to lose — were now recorded.

My journal has become an instrument of my survival, helping me to reintegrate my life. From time to time, I leaf through the pages. As I reread sections of happier

moments, I laugh aloud at half-forgotten incidents. Then there are those painful moments of anguish, quiet, and emptiness. I realize how far I have come since those terrible times. I no longer experience the clutch of internal agony in my stomach.

It is now almost two years since my beloved mother died. I have traversed the stages of grief, reached acceptance, and am building a new life for myself. But in writing this essay, I am suddenly confronted with feelings that I had earlier denied and camouflaged. I realize that the pain of separation is never over.

My journal has lost some of its importance. I no longer write every day. Nevertheless, it is still a special friend to have around. I know that I can be honest with my feelings. My friends can see behind my mask and still love me. With their help and now my writings, the event of my mother's death will continue to be a source of learning and growth. Perhaps, like my mother, I can now help others.

Roberta Decker

On December 8, 1964, Samuel M. Levinson died at the age of 74.

His son, Aaron, worked closely with his father in the family business. Aaron was able to avoid the idealization that often takes place after death and confront his bruised, conflicting emotions honestly. Themes from earlier periods in the family history were replayed. Aaron responded with jealousy, guilt, sadness — and relief. After some of the former hurts in the father-son relationship were resolved, he began to view the association more objectively. "My dad was not perfect, yet some of his imperfections, along with his deep insight, made him very human and very lovable . . . He could make you laugh and he could make you cry . . . He was my dad."

A SON'S FEELINGS
ABOUT HIS FATHER'S DEATH

Memories Never Die

When my father died, I was besieged with conflicting thoughts and feelings. He was no ordinary man, and ours was no ordinary relationship. He was a powerful and dominant person, loved by many, feared by a few, but unnoticed by no one. His qualities seemed sometimes contradictory. He was a caring person, yet sometimes insensitive. He had an agile mind and was brilliant in many areas, and yet at times, the most obvious things escaped him. He had a deep understanding of human nature and was responsive to human needs all over the world; yet sometimes he understood nothing about the feelings of people very close to him.

I had a deep love and admiration for my dad all my life, and yet I could never tell him. I know he also had a deep love for me, but he could never show affection.

Until I was twelve or thirteen, I called him Daddy, but after that, I couldn't even say Dad. During our years together in the family business, I sometimes called him S.M. Sometimes, I just started talking without calling him anything. The one or two times I tried calling him Dad or Daddy, it was awkward for both of us, and I didn't try anymore.

Once when I was fourteen, I ran all the way home from football practice because I knew he would be there after a week out of town. As I burst into the house, he grabbed me because he had received a bad report about me from my mother and took me down to the cellar, took off his belt and gave me a whipping. I went upstairs and lay face down on my bed. My mother came to me, tears in her eyes, helped me take off my shirt and put cold compresses on the welts that covered my back. The hurt ran deep inside me, but I did not shed a tear. While that episode may have intensified the conflicts I had about my dad, I don't think it changed my feelings for him. I loved him very much, but I could never be relaxed in his company or express my love until many years later.

It was during a period of illness just a few months before my dad's death that he and I, for the first time since my early childhood, displayed and expressed genuine love for each other. I had already begun to deal with my feelings about him on a psychiatrist's couch. My mother had often thought about the beating I received from my father when I was a child and wanted the three of us to talk about it while he was still alive. Knowing the end was near for my dad, she brought up the subject one day as we sat on the edge of my dad's bed. With his face pulled to the side and his speech slurred as a result of his stroke, he put his arms around me and said, "I'm sorry, Aaron. I love you very much." I said, "I'm sorry too, Dad. I love you." Then, all three of us cried.

When I was thirty-five and he was fifty-eight, he suggested to his brothers, who made up the board of directors of our family company, that I become president of the company and that he be elected chairman of the board. My uncles accepted this suggestion and I became president and chief operating officer in the growing family company. As sometimes happens in these family situations, my father seemed to have ambivalent feelings about my ability and my success. He had always been head of the family and the family business, and he found it difficult to accept someone else doing the job or adjusting to different or better ways. My dad did not have the temperament to sit by as a kind of elder statesman. He took pride in my ability, but it just wasn't in him to let me do the job while he acted as a counselor. A few years after I became the president, my dad began asserting himself, as he had when *he* was president. This was a very difficult period for me, because he was making all the decisions or countermanding mine, leaving me in no-man's land. Although this is not unusual in a father-son business relationship, I deeply resented the change. There were times when part of me wanted him to die or at least part of me was saying, "When my father dies, all of this will change."

After he had his stroke things did, of course, change. Even then, I began to have guilt feelings about some of those earlier thoughts. He loved his business and was a man of great will. With the help of a nurse, an elevator, and a special rigging to get him in and out of his car, he managed to get to his office almost every day. He did this for years. He loved to look over the orders and talk to the managers. One day, when he finished with his two hours in his office, he asked his nurse to wheel him into my office and then dismissed her. Again, with his face pulled to the side and his slurred speech he said, "Aaron, this is it." I said, "What do you mean?" He said, "I have had it. I'm going to die." I tried to make light of it, but I knew down deep, he had given up. The next day, he died.

Even though he had been ill for a long time, his death was a shock to me. I loved him so very much. I had guilt feelings about my earlier fantasies about his health. I also vividly recalled the scene in his bedroom with my mother, and I couldn't forget that just the day before, he had given up and had said he was going to die.

In spite of these deep and pent-up feelings, I was not able to cry at the time of his death. I had been able to deal with and express many of my feelings on the psychiatrist's couch during the preceding years, but somehow, when my father died, my way of dealing with his death was not with tears. I felt that some members of my family thought I was very callous. Just the opposite was true. I have been told that each person handles grief in his or her own way. Mine came out in incessant sobbing in my dreams for years after my father's death.

If there was one thing that helped me to accept the reality of my father's death, it was reflecting on his life. He meant so much to so many people. He was a man with deep principles. His life really stood for something. My dad's been dead for more than fifteen years, and yet almost every day I think of some philosophy, some idea, some principle, or some lesson of life I learned from him. My dad was not perfect, yet some of his imperfections, along with his deep insight, made him very human and very lovable.

Another thing that sustained and gave me strength at the time of his death was recognizing that my dad's life was a success. Those who knew him best, his family and close friends, know that the world is a little better because he lived. He built a business; he was a community leader;

he did so much for his family; and he added a little humor and a better sense of values to every life he touched.

Even during the long period after his stroke, he didn't allow people to take his illness too seriously. Sometimes, when people asked how he felt, he would reply, "The doctor said I'll never die!" Then with a twinkle in his eye, he would add, "As long as I live!" Or he might say, "The doctor said I would have a complete recovery." Then, he would pause and smile and add, "If I live long enough."

I think if my dad had been another kind of guy, if his life had been a failure, if he had not left me such a rich heritage, I might have handled his death quite differently. But, even though I felt a great sadness, the memories of his life and what he had stood for gave me the strength to accept his death and to carry on his work in the company, in the community, and in the family.

Now, some sixteen years after his death, as I begin to approach the age my father was when he became sick, I think I have learned to look at his life more objectively. True, he wasn't perfect, but he could also be a giant, a hero and a person of whom I was in awe. At this point in my life, I can relate more closely to some of his feelings and think of him neither as an insensitive man nor as an unapproachable saint, but instead as a wonderful human being — a guy with strengths and weaknesses, with lots of warmth, lots of feelings and lots of love. He could make you laugh and he could make you cry. Underneath, he was just a plain, terrific guy. He was my dad.

Aaron P. Levinson

On October 22, 1979, Bella Brief died after a five-year confinement in a nursing home.

Her son, Rabbi Neil Brief, recounts his feelings at different stages of the mourning process: a day after her funeral, five months later, and six months later. He guides the reader through the Jewish ceremonies of death. The *Shiva* refers to the first seven days of intensive mourning. *Sh'loshim,* meaning "thirty," includes an additional twenty-three days where the bereaved resume normal activity, but avoid places of entertainment. At the *Minyan* (daily worship) and the Sabbath services, the mourner reads aloud for a period of eleven months the *Kaddish* ("Holy") prayer. This Aramaic liturgy is a pledge to dedicate one's life to the God of Life "Magnified and Sanctified." The *Yahrzeit* is the anniversary of death where *Kaddish* is again said and a memorial light is kindled in the home. The memorial prayer of *Yiskor* ("May God remember the soul of the revered") is recited four times a year during a Jewish holiday in the synagogue worship.

Responses to shock and grief are structured by defined solemn procedures. Mourners are not to suppress memories, even disturbing ones, even guilt-provoking recollections which are an inevitable part of all human relations. In Rabbi Brief's words, "It is not easy to turn a new page and forget the old one written in love, caring, and sharing." Jews, including rabbis, mourn.

RABBIS DO MOURN

The Courage to Continue

October 23, 1979

I don't know how else to say it. A surgeon once boasted and wrote a novel called *Surgeons Don't Cry* and I was both pleased and envious at the same time. Now, at my mother's death, as I observe the prescribed seven-day period of mourning, Shiva, I mourn, deeply and fully as I try to come to grips with the reality of no more daily phone calls and no more visits to the nursing home where Mom lived for the past five years.

I reflect upon the years devoted to rabbinic service here and how intertwined Mom's life was with ours. Mom was widowed in April 1961 when I had just become a U.S. Army chaplain at Fort Huachuca, Arizona. In the ten years, our lives — Erica's, mine, and our three children's, Dena, David, and Debbie — had become jet-plane, phone-and-letter-and-visit connected. We worked hard at continuing the relationship with Mom and in the process crisscrossed the country. When I was a chaplain in Arizona, a rabbi in Ventura, California, and later in Skokie, Illinois, we lived, kept in touch, communicated, maintained family ties, and cherished the years.

Now Mom is dead and buried and I must pick up the pieces and go on. Yet, it is not so easy to turn a new page and forget the old ones written in love, caring, and sharing, for rabbis do mourn. During the Shiva period, a visitor who came to call was startled with his newly discovered insight. He just couldn't believe that rabbis do mourn. He, himself, had lost his wife a few short weeks ago and was deep in mourning when he heard of my mother's death. He joined a Minyan, a gathering of worshipers at my home to recite Kaddish, the memorial prayer, and then, upon leaving sought to console me with this revelation, suddenly aware that even rabbis do mourn. Yes, I do.

I mourn for the what-might-have-been-but-never-was. I mourn for the years of life in which questions of purpose, meaning, pain, love, and existence go unanswered. I mourn for childhood, youth, maturity, and old age, which even when lived fully now seem so incomplete. I mourn for the passing of my mother's mother in Europe, which caused my mother to be in between two families and compelled her to be self-sufficient at an early age. She made her way from Russia to America as a twenty-one-year-old woman alone, and yet determined to make it, in a vibrant, post–World War I Brooklyn community. I mourn for great-uncles, aunts, and cousins who remained in Europe to perish in the Holocaust and for others who, like my mother, were able to die with love and dignity. I mourn for a lifetime lived in airtight compartments of time and space, memories and hopes, purposes and possibilities. I mourn for my father's debilitating illness, confinement, institutionalization, and ultimate death. My mother's role became one that is increasingly common today, a parent without partner.

It was in Skokie that my mother decided to live her last days. After my father's death, my mother lived periods of time with us in both Arizona and California, but in 1968, settled in Miami Beach for the next six years while we, in turn, moved from California to Skokie in 1971. We celebrated Mom's seventieth birthday with her in 1969 in Miami Beach, just five days before man first walked the moon; marked her seventy-fifth birthday in Skokie in 1974, just a few short days before Nixon's Watergate resignation; Mom's eightieth birthday in 1979 was lived in a summer of cabinet resignations, inflationary uncertainties, the excitement of a papal visit to Chicago and, above all else, a five-week hospitalization prior to her last days at the nursing home.

I ask then, for so many years lived, why do I mourn? I mourn because of a sense of gratitude, debt, and understanding I was privileged to experience and can experience no more.

In a world where formal degrees are the prerequisites for position and power and where I too have earned several of them, my mother, on my forty-fifth birthday, conferred the greatest degree upon me by calling me — my son!

Mom was failing — the doctor, sensitive, and yet hoping, as we did, against hope, called her condition stable. We visited daily. It was during Sukkut, Feast of Tabernacles, and my birthday, which a year ago was celebrated on the eve of Yom Kippur, the Day of Atonement. I went to the hospital to see Mom and wish her well on what I called her birth-day. Mom was not eating; the tubes were going full blast. I shared the knowledge of her birth-day forty-five years before, and she remained quiet, stable — no comment. I asked, "Mom, do you know who I am?" — No response! "Mom, do you know who I am?" — Again, no response. I had hoped she would simply say my name — Neil. Again, I asked her to identify me. Then, as if by miracle and miracle alone it must remain, Mom spoke and said, "my son." Shortly afterward she died and now I will no longer hear the words "my son" from my mother's lips. They were spoken from one heart to another — a mother to a son — and they will remain with me for a lifetime.

The prophet Malachi, as if speaking for the prophet Elijah, best said it when he spoke of a Messianic Age, when the hearts of children will be turned to parents and the hearts of parents will be turned to children and the words *my son, my mother,* will echo and resound with love in greater amplification than ever before.

For the lack of that, I mourn and for the realization of that prophecy, I dream on and continue.

March 20, 1980

Days after my mother died, I wrote the above article, called "Rabbis Do Mourn," in her memory. Now, five months later I ask myself: "Where have these days gone and how have I responded to them? What lessons have I learned and what can I share with others?" First I shed a tear. I shed a tear when in the morning service I recited the first of four memorial prayers for my mother. I was truly sad that she could not be with us to share my nephew's Bar Mitzvah (thirteenth birthday) this morning and the celebration for him tonight.

Those we love the most cannot be us and we cannot be them. How very limited we really are. We may remember and cherish and love beyond the grave, but we cannot bring back those who are dead and gone. I remember watching at the graveside as the coffin was lowered into the ground and dirt had to be shoveled. It was so final, almost a nightmare. I wanted to wake up. Mom — immortal Mom — had died! I knew she had to die, but when she did, it just could not be. Even now, it is hard to come to grips with it. Mom is dead — I write it and know it, but it feels as if she is away and will return one day soon.

I look in my brother's wedding album, almost eighteen years old. Mom is vibrant and alert and so pleased and proud. She would have been as pleased and proud today. She last saw the Bar Mitzvah boy when he visited her at the nursing home where she quite literally held court. Her wheelchair was her throne and from it she earned the respect of everyone with whom she had contact.

Mom's last five years in the nursing home were the final chapter in a life that spanned eighty years in Europe and in the United States. She arrived in New York at twenty-one, unable to speak the language, but blessed with a determination to learn. In a marriage fraught with illness and sadness, she persevered, raising my brother and me, from whom she was blessed with six grandchildren. Her last twenty years were filled with sunshine, sunset, twilight, and night! Travels to Russia, in America, from coast to coast, and fulfilling a lifetime dream, two visits to Israel, were among the peaks. It is when I write and recall her life that I feel strengthened and comforted. Mom may not live anymore, but the miracle is that once she did live and out of her living example, I am privileged to emerge. She is the tree from which my brother and I and our dear ones branch out. We are not meant to live forever but we are here for a purpose and we are links in a chain of family. My mother was daughter to Chaim, and Chaim a son of Pesach. My brother and I are sons of Bella and in turn are privileged to be parents. I ponder the flow and the tasks that challenge us to cope and continue. I want to live until I die. I want to cherish everyone who is a part of my life in such a way that through memory, eternity is never an alien concept. Each day is a gift and each one with whom we are privileged to share is a bonus. Nothing or no one can ever be taken for granted. Those who give us life and inspire us teach us how special we are and show us the circle of life in which we are bound. I cope by remembering the good times, the possibilities, the hope. I come to grips with the sadness by recognizing the inevitability and the glory and greatness that come from it!

It is said that time heals, and so it does. Mom died in the fall and today is spring. In between has been the winter. Where we live winter is cold; there is severe snow, rain, ice, and sleet, perhaps all reminiscent of death. Death, like difficult weather, tests our endurability. We want to endure, especially with those who mean so much to us, but we need to learn to let go and let be. Death is the grand finale, the curtain call, the concluding blessing, and if all else leading up to it has been special, our lives deserve a standing ovation. Each time I recite the Kaddish, I stand. It is the standing ovation for a life performance second to none! It is our Jewish way of notifying both friend and stranger of those whom we love who shall never be forgotten.

How has grief affected me as a rabbi? Perhaps I am more sensitized to the suffering of others, having had my share. Personal loss teaches me anew how central is my calling and outreach. As I reach out to others, so, too, do others respond more fully to me. Their reaching out uplifts and inspires and I become more of the person I want to be. It's an unexpected blessing grown out of grief — the last of Mom's many gifts to me.

April 7, 1980

I shall soon officiate at the first Yiskor Memorial Service since my mother, Bella Brief, of blessed memory, died.

Though almost six months have passed, my mother's memory is still very warm.

Following her death, after the seven days of Shiva I began to resume my rabbinic duties, but with a different slant. There was an emptiness, a void, a chasm, a glaring hole. I began to feel like a total parent, no longer a child. I sought to fine-tune my Judaism and specifically the recitation of the Kaddish prayer affirming life even as it remembers and honors the departed. At times I would become dismayed at those in the synagogue who so totally neglected the duties I sometimes assumed for them as a rabbi, duties I considered a privilege to perform. There were times I wanted to go to another synagogue, incognito, to honor my mother's memory so that others would not simply think it was automatic for me as a rabbi to recite Kaddish. I remember the Shabbat eve services during the week of Shiva. I was told by one of our synagogue leaders that if I did not come or officiate everyone would

115

understand. But I simply had to be at the synagogue and lead the service. After all wasn't that what Mom would have wanted? Isn't that what I had been trained for? And it was the thirty-second anniversary of my Bar Mitzvah and how could I do honor to the memory of an event Mom worked so hard to make possible, except to celebrate and to cherish it?

The same evening was the Bar Mitzvah of a young man whose Dad had died tragically fifteen months before. I had to be there and share. It was not easy but when I took note of that courageous mother who was so determined, I saw a glimpse of my mother's life as well. That determination, that persistence, that perseverance: It was the story of her life.

The day Mom was buried my brother, Sy, and I shoveled the dirt over her grave and, standing together like the two trees that adorn her grave, across the road from the bronze Torah-like scroll on a rock, we recited Kaddish. After the Shiva period concluded, I went to the nursing home to gather together Mom's belongings. They were simple, few, limited. By material standards, Mom would not be ranked among any of the *Fortune* 500. Yet she died with a good name and with love. O what love. She had lived at Terrace Nursing Home in Skokie, Illinois, for over five years. The decision to live there was not an easy one to make. At times I wondered if it had been right. Mom would not, could not, walk; her pain-racked body found comfort in a wheelchair and in a bed. Even when I brought her to our home, as I did every Shabbat eve, just the short walk from the driveway to the side door entrance with the aid of a walker was a step-by-step process. If I could have lain down on the ground to make it easier for her, I would have, but I could not. With the responsibilities of a busy household, three growing teenagers and a vital, dynamic congregation, I just couldn't do everything.

Now I am in the coping stage! It is not a one-time challenge, but rather an ongoing one. As a delegate to a national synagogue convention in New York during *Sh'loshim,* the thirty-day second stage period of mourning, I regularly attended every worship service and stood up to be counted. The comfort of other people from all over the United States and overseas and the sensitivity shown in tender expression and friendly awareness was a balm to my wounded heart. The pain of loss is hard to bear, but when shared, a new understanding deeper than before emerges.

In a five-month period, beginning in August, I lost my mother, an uncle, a long-time friend, a very special former congregant, a rabbinic professor, a step-grandmother, and an aunt. Seven deaths in such a short period of time! I prepare for the Yiskor Memorial Service. It is one of four such services held throughout the year and together with the Yahrzeit, or anniversary of death, recalls the memory of those beloved whose lives are intertwined with ours. Gone but not forgotten — the daily recitations help. Gone but not forgotten — the letters, cards, donations, tributes, and expressions of love and friendship are all a tremendous comfort. Prayers and meditations written by others are clearer in their meaning. I am more committed to study now than before. I am grateful to Elisabeth Kübler-Ross for what at the time was an academic workshop in death and dying, but now becomes a vital force in coping and continuing.

I return from time to time to the nursing home to celebrate Shabbat, Chanukah, and Passover. When ask-d how I can when my mother is no longer living there, I answer that my mother still lives in the hearts of those who would gather around her for a timely word, a thoughtful gesture, an encouraging smile. When I am helpful to my children, I am translating my mother's influence upon me into the lives of our children. Soon it will be my father's nineteenth Yahrzeit. Two days later, we will commemorate the Holocaust, or Yom Ha Shoah, cherishing the memory of the six million Jews who were ruthlessly murdered by the Nazis. I am reminded of the sign in the pool where our children first learned to swim THERE IS NO GAIN WITHOUT PAIN. Life is loss and pain and yet the courage to cope and continue. I learned this lesson when I visited Dachau's infamous concentration camp on August 4, 1959, and before its crematoria, vowed not to grant a posthumous victory to Hitler, to become a rabbi, a teacher of Judaism. I learned this lesson in standing up and speaking out at both my father's and mother's funerals, eighteen and a half years apart and affirming the purpose of their existence in my being, as I pray one day my children will do in recalling my memory for blessing.

Soon I shall conclude my twentieth year as a rabbi, which will be highlighted by a dinner and shortly thereafter by leading a synagogue pilgrimage to Israel. In anticipation of these occasions and in the spirit in which I look forward to their celebration, I had the privilege of sharing a nephew's Bar Mitzvah, one of my brother's three children, one of the six grandchildren with whom my mother was blessed. Joseph Benjamin, as he is called, flew in from Miami Beach to visit my mother for what was to be the last time, in May 1979. Not having seen her for several years due to moves and distances, Joey was quickly taken by Mom's smile and tenderness. He proceeded in all his innocence to tell her how he never knew he had a *bubbe* (Yiddish for "grandmother") like her! As I watched Joseph Benjamin assume the mantle of becoming a responsible Jewish adult and remembered the names of the persons for whom he was named in blessed memory, I realized anew the cycle, ongoing and continuing in life, from generation to generation. In name, in influence, in deed, and in our lives, those, such as parents who give us life, are continued. *They are continued* and in such affirmation do we cope. We cope and we continue and therein are blessed. May the memory of my parents ever be for blessing.

Neil Brief

WHAT HELPED
When Others Die

When a friend dies, you lose a piece of yourself.

Members of the family are not the only ones who grieve. Friends and helpers — teachers, clergy, physicians, nurses, psychologists, funeral directors, physical therapists, and social workers grieve too. They also feel the pain of loss, the feelings of denial, despair, and guilt. They, too, are saddened and angered by those things that cannot be changed. Death is often accepted as the opposite of success, synonymous with failure and defeat. To show emotion is not to lose objectivity and professionalism. Being human, it is natural to shed a tear and allow a sigh of distress. Being around death brings up thoughts of one's own mortality. Not enough attention has been given to the psychological well-being of those involved in the helping professions. Professionals have their needs. "Who," they often wonder, "takes care of the caregiver?"

In seventh grade, Glen was diagnosed as having leukemia. Midway through the eighth grade, he died.

The principal of the school, Dr. Eliot Levinson; a student, Steven Ham; the school nurse, Jean Sutherland; and the physical therapist, Betsy Greenstein, all share their feelings over Glen's illness and death.

The common theme is the principal's words: "I think schools do have a role in dealing with the death of a student, one of acknowledgment, mourning, and commemoration."

DEATH COMES
TO AN EIGHTH-GRADER

Reflections that Wound and Comfort

Principal

In March 1979, Glen's father, George Gledhill, came to school to see me, visibly upset. He told me his son had been diagnosed as having leukemia and that 80 percent

of those who had this form of leukemia survived. We discussed how Glen would gradually move back to school after he gained some of his strength back and went into remission. He knew little about the disease, but shared some literature with me. I gave him a copy of Doris Lund's *Eric,* a mother's account of her son's life and death from leukemia.

Toward the end of the school year, Glen came back to school. We moved him into the eighth grade, although his attendance had been minimal since he was regaining his strength during the spring. At the end of the summer, Mrs. Gledhill and I discussed the arrangements. She wanted Glen to be treated as a normal student, as much as possible and, other than not taking physical education, be able to go about his business at the junior high school. I offered the Gledhills tutorial services for Glen and the possibility of having a two-way telephone between their home and the school. The Gledhills did not expect to need the phone service, but said they would use the tutorial as necessary. I talked with Glen, too, who very much wanted to be treated as a normal kid, with no visible fuss made over him. When he did come to school, he wore a baseball hat over his bald head and kids didn't give him a hard time.

When Glen first became sick, there was a big rush of cards and visits from the other students and then it all dropped off to nothing by the end of the school year. Two weeks into the new school year, Glen had a relapse and stopped attending school for what we thought at that time would be a temporary period. In about mid-October, I began contacting Mrs. Gledhill on a fairly regular basis, to see how Glen was doing, and dropped in to bring him books. I believed, despite his relapse, that things would get better, and I found it fairly easy to call to check on

how he was doing and to discuss the situation with his teachers.

During this time, we arranged for two key teachers to visit Glen at home and tutor him in his subjects. We also arranged to have the two-way telephone system installed so that Glen could be "present at school" while sitting at home. During October and November, Glen had a lot of pain and bad reactions to chemotherapy. He couldn't use the phone service, but he did take advantage of the tutoring when he was able. Toward late fall or early winter, Glen appeared to be improving considerably and, although he was now confined to a wheelchair, he appeared at school one day. It was one of the first places he wanted to go when he got out of the hospital. I remember being thrilled to see him wheeling into the office and arranging to have one of his friends take him around the school the next day. It was a very special day and I kind of felt the excitement that Glen was going to turn the corner. At this time, I sat down and had a long talk with Glen about what would have to be done to help him make it through the school year. I told him that I really couldn't expect the day-to-day work from him, but we would figure out what were the essences of courses and make sure that he got enough work done so that he could comfortably move on to high school next year, having legitimately completed the eighth grade.

At first, Glen resisted the thought of having to do work again, but within a day or two he decided he wanted to settle down into the school year. He was tutored regularly and he made use of the two-way telephone, which his classmates took from class to class so he could plug in.

In early December members of the Wayland Parmenter Health Center and I attended a meeting at Children's Hospital for school and agency professionals who were working with kids with leukemia. In the session, run by parents of children with leukemia and Children's Hospital social workers, it was suggested that a successful strategy was to treat the child as normal, understand that he's different, and follow the lead of the child and the family about what they were and were not able to do. The session was beneficial for me because it confirmed with a professional imprimatur that we'd been heading in the right direction. I was always wondering whether we were doing enough for Glen or whether we were treating him *too much* as an invalid.

During the fall, Glen's contact with kids had dropped off. People stopped sending him cards after his initial bout in the hospital and very few kids went to see him. We spoke to a few kids and three or four started going over to see him on a regular basis. Around Christmastime, it became obvious that Glen was critically ill. He was not going to live. Although I could see how ill he was, I really could not believe that he would die. What was most helpful to me was my work with the visiting nurse, who both tended to the Gledhills and worked in the school. Being able to check in with her about his illness helped me understand what was happening. From January on, Glen was no longer coming to school. He continued his contact with his tutors when possible and a few close teachers and I visited him from time to time.

The times I visited Glen in February and March, I sat in the living room with him and talked about what was happening at school or in the neighborhood. His family was always around and sometimes some of Glen's friends would drop by. One time, two of the boys from the junior high school were there. I was struck at how being alive really means the nitty-gritty common things that we take for granted. They talked about going to the movies, what they ate for dinner, and who got detention today. I was also struck by the power of a family to take care of itself through an event like the death of a child. The Gledhills kept up a massive barrage of normalcy in talking with each other. They were talking to Glen as though he were going to be around for a long time; though he was lying down on the couch, too weak to sit up, clearly close to death. I was particularly amazed at how his mother was with him constantly, in the house or taking him to the hospital. She was omnipresent, his spokesperson.

During the hard winter period, Glen's four or five close friends visited him daily or nearly so. Sitting around the Gledhill living room, they talked about what was happening in Boy Scouts, who got into problems with the school office, or who was doing what. I think that they allowed Glen to keep functioning and yet I was amazed at how they could handle the thing so normally, with much less strain than I could when faced with this very emaciated and terribly ill boy. The pathos of the situation did not seem to dawn on them. I had nothing but incredible respect for how they were acting with Glen over the last two months of his life.

During February, Glen and his family went to the Olympics together and this seemed to provide Glen with an incredible high; he was able to live out a dream that he had. When he came back from the Olympics, he was relaxed but excited and more animated than I had ever heard him.

The end came very quickly. The beginning of March, I spoke to Mrs. Gledhill who told me that the doctor had told both Glen and her that Glen would be dead in two weeks. At that point, I decided to go see Glen and visited him twice during that period, checking in, also, by phone. I also became, at that point, very concerned with dealing with the death of a fourteen-year-old boy in a school setting. I understood that most junior-high-age kids still think of themselves as immortal. How Glen's death was handled with the staff and students would be very important. Consulting with other school principals, I found out they really did not have much experience with death in the school, and there were no models to follow. We'd just have to work out our own ways. The day after Glen died, I got hold of his five close friends to see how they were functioning. It took time for them to just talk about Glen and to vent their feelings. Some of the kids were very shocked and some were quickly able to reminisce about the good times that they had with Glen. In the school as a whole, there was an immediate contagious pall. Kids were visibly shaken over the death, even though Glen had, for all practical purposes, not been in school for a year and many people had not known him. The day after Glen's death, I gathered the seventh- and eighth-grade classes separately and informed them of Glen's death. I told them that those who wanted to go, could walk over to the funeral together during the school day or that they could go with their families. I told them not to feel they should mourn if they hadn't known Glen, but to do what was comfortable if they had known him. I took about forty-five minutes with the faculty going over Glen's illness and death and talking about ways to be available to kids who wanted to talk, since death would be a very important topic on their minds.

The day of the funeral, approximately two hundred students, or 40 percent of the school, walked over to the funeral together. This was followed by small discussion groups with teachers to enable students to talk about what was on their minds: either about death or about Glen. These groups were extremely functional. Students talked about their own fears about mortality, they talked about the injustice of Glen's dying, and about how hard and long he had suffered. After the small groups, which lasted for one class period, students went about their business and the crying and upset of the previous days seemed to lift.

I talked with four boys in my small group who were very close to Glen. The kids talked about how they found out he had died, how they felt, and also about a lot of the good times they had had together in the woods camping and snowmobiling. They also discussed their disbelief that he was dead. We all talked together of what life had been like for Glen over the last couple of months when he had been so obviously ill.

Glen Gledhill was someone I would never have known very well if he hadn't gotten sick. He was an extremely hard-working, serious student. He wasn't going to be a star in the play or end up in my office for behavioral problems. He was one of those solid, good kids whom I would have known by face and name only. He was a "boy's boy"; his passion was Boy Scouts and his primary group was his Scout troop. His interests centered more on Scouts than on school. Only when his family sought me out for the educational resources he needed did I really get to know him. I have some mixed feelings about this year. On the one hand, I feel that I did not see Glen enough, or get to know him well enough, and I have the sense that there is probably more that I and the school could have done. On the other hand, I think that there were some things that were done well for Glen. His illness, his life, and his death were very much acknowledged. We provided the educational resources that he needed and we also checked in with him on a regular basis in a very personal way through three or four staff members and four or five kids who saw him. We kept in contact with him throughout his illness.

Seeing Glen in the last several months was a powerful experience for me. He made me realize that there is something very special in everybody and that you do have a lot of control in living out your life, as tragic and limited as it can be at age fourteen. Glen had a great sense of humor; he was properly feisty about things like school-work and he did things like taking an eighteen-mile bike hike in October and going to the Olympics, which took a great deal of strength. He very rarely complained about the pain and the problems of his illness. It was amazing to see that kind of strength in a fourteen-year-old.

It was not easy to call up Mrs. Gledhill or go to see Glen. Especially in the beginning and middle of his illness. It was one of those things I wanted to avoid. I found it easier to make the effort toward the end. I really wanted to see Glen to make sure that in whatever limited way possible, he was helped fully to live out what he wanted to. As time went on, I developed an affection for Glen and enjoyed him very much.

On reflection, I do think that the school handled Glen's illness and death fairly well. Perhaps students should have seen him more, but they *did* see him, and neither ignored him nor went overboard. Particularly when he died, I think we did a good job attending to the concerns of other teenagers and the staff who knew him. Schools do have a role in dealing with the death of a student; one of acknowledgment, mourning, and commemoration. I'm pleased that we were able to carry out that role in such a positive way.

Eliot Levinson
Principal,
Wayland Junior High School

Nurse

As the new junior high school nurse, I just became aware of Glen Gledhill's illness during the summer of his remission. In August, I called the Gledhill's to ask about his condition. He was stable, but was being seen regularly at Children's Hospital Medical Center (CHMC). His plan was to return to school in September. Glen did attend the first day of school, but never again returned to studies in the classroom.

In September, when I noticed his frequent absences from school, I called his home and learned that the chemotherapy was leaving him very weak, nauseated, unable to eat, and, of course, unable to come to school. Mrs. Gledhill hoped that at some point he would be able to return. I offered to make a home nursing visit, but Mrs. Gledhill said that she thought Glen might feel such a visit meant that he was very sick. She came instead to the health center where I work to discuss Glen's illness. Each time we met she needed about half an hour to talk about details of Glen's blood and chemical profile and about events that had occurred at CHMC. Then I could ask her how *she* was doing and she could tell me what was really going on with her, with Glen, and with the rest of the family. She was always very open; genuinely angry, hurt, depressed, frustrated, afraid, and bewildered by all that was happening to her and her family. Throughout the year her major question was, "Why?" Why her son, why her, why the confusion at CHMC, why the continuous relapses, why the ups and downs, and finally, why did her son die. I could provide no answers, but I could be a sounding board, a supporter, a coordinator between school and home, and a community resource.

I never tried to make her bare her soul to me nor did I try to push her to face the facts of Glen's prognosis, but as the months progressed these topics did come up. I let Mrs. Gledhill lead the discussion and just listened. At times I was frustrated by being such a passive participant in our conversations. I wanted to offer words of wisdom or concrete advice or direction, but there was very little that I could say. Glen never responded to chemotherapy or radiation. His illness only got worse. It left him completely paralyzed from his waist down and limited his use of his left hand. Both Glen and the family were angry and frustrated because it was obvious that he really was sick. He lost his hair from the chemotherapy and this, coupled with his marked weight loss and inability to walk without help, left him with a very negative body image.

Glen never gave up trying and neither did his family. They were willing to try anything that they thought might help. The physical therapist from our clinic saw Glen daily in an effort to help him walk independently. I would monitor Glen's vital signs and talked with him about school. Our conversations were never long, but I hoped that my visits would help him feel that "the school" cared about him and had not forgotten him. On my visits, I would check both Mr. and Mrs. Gledhill's blood pressure and offer advice to them on diet, rest, and activity, so that they could stay healthy throughout this stressful time.

My conversations with Mr. Gledhill were quite a contrast to those with Mrs. Gledhill. He poured out his innermost feelings to me. Often he would be in tears while we talked. He was very angry, frustrated, and hurt and felt inadequate in trying to help his wife and son through this time. Mr. Gledhill was instrumental in planning a trip that the family took to the Winter Olympics. It was to be Glen's last trip away from home. He was proud and pleased that he had been able to organize this trip for Glen.

As school nurse, my role was as supporter to the family, community resource, and health supervisor while Glen was at home. After Glen's death I called and saw his family daily. We continue to meet monthly as they go through this first year adjusting to their loss.

Jean Sutherland

Physical Therapist

I saw Glen perhaps eight or nine times for physical therapy. Using exercises to strengthen weakened muscles and practice in walking to build up endurance, we tried to help him function as well as he could for as long as his disease allowed.

It's one thing to invest yourself in a sure thing. It's quite another to involve yourself when the outcome is so uncertain — even bleak. Glen and I talked about this and concluded that "In whatever you do, you should give it your best shot." Talking it through helped Glen make the decision to work with me, even when he was not feeling very well.

It was not Glen alone who needed attention. His mother, as his primary caregiver, needed to talk and I listened as she told me of all the latest tests, their results, and the new plans for treatment. She shared with me the feelings that she, Glen, and the family had about Glen's illness. There was a strong desire to fight periodically mixed with the fear of "what if."

Sadly, "what if" became "when." In March 1980, Glen and his family lost the battle they had fought so courageously to win.

Betsy Greenstein

Fellow Student

I knew Glen for about four years. Glen used to play with my brother; then he started to hang around with Scott, Paul, and me. We did many things together. Scott, Glen, and I were on the same baseball team — the Mets. Once when we had a game Scott and Glen were late. Then a big camper drove up and beeped the horn — and there they were! That night we slept in the camper.

Glen liked to ride his motorcycle everywhere. I wanted to buy a bike, but I didn't have enough money. My brother said he'd buy it. That night was the night we found out that Glen was sick. Around supper time I got a telephone call from Glen. "Hey, Steve," he said. "I'm in the Boston hospital and I have leukemia." I said, "You must be kidding." But he wasn't.

I was stunned by the news. Glen was in the hospital for a month and a half and we all went to see him. It was a sad sight to see all the people in bed sick.

Then Glen came home from the hospital. He had to go back for treatments about once a month. We did a lot of things together like camping and dirt-bike riding.

Glen's condition got very bad. I was worried that he was going to die. I would stop every day on my paper route to see Glen. One day I found out that Glen was paralyzed on the left side. Then one Sunday I delivered a paper to Glen's aunt and she said, "Do you know Glen?" I said, "Yes." She said, "Well, he passed away this morning." I was in shock. I went to Glen's house and found out that it was true. I went to tell Paul, but he already knew. Paul, Jeff, and I walked all morning thinking about it.

Sometimes we talk about the good times we had together — and the things Glen did. One of the best things was that Glen got to go to the Olympics just before he died. But we still feel bad. It is very sad to see one of your best friends die. It is very frightening, too.

Steven Ham

J immy, a man of twenty-two, lingered five days in a coma as a result of a drug overdose. He died without regaining consciousness.

A priest who had counseled Jimmy describes his feelings when he learns of the death. A clergyman is foremost a human person. "But prayer was no easy proposition." He experienced guilt, denial, and anger. "Anger at myself, anger at Jimmy — even anger at God." It is difficult for those in the helping professions "to be reminded of the limitations of our fragile humanity."

Eight years later, this priest reviews how Jimmy's death and his Christian faith help to "look for answers to the unanswerable questions . . . to try to make sense out of senseless tragedy."

Reverend Rodney J. Copp, currently an associate pastor of Saint Joseph Parish, Belmont, Massachusetts, and chaplain to the Massachusetts Police Association, is particularly interested in pastoral counseling aspects of the ministry.

A PRIEST REFLECTS ON THE DEATH OF A PARISHIONER

Remembrance Is a Form of Meeting

It has been eight years — almost — and yet with surprising clarity I recall the day I learned of Jimmy's death. It was one of those glorious late October days; the air was cool but not cold, the sun warm and penetrating, and the leaves bright with reds and golds.

I was in my last year of seminary in that October of 1972, looking forward to the completion of eight long years of education. The previous May I had been ordained a deacon and sent out to do parish ministry. The last two years of school had been a combination of theological studies and field work: the first in ministry to alcoholic and drug-dependent people in a small detoxification and rehabilitation facility, the second ministering to the chronically and terminally ill at Youville Hospital in Cambridge, Massachusetts. I considered myself fortunate to have had the opportunity of working for two years in clinical settings, where most of my interest was concentrated. Parish life was a new adventure — a final year of internship to prepare me for ordination to the priesthood in May 1973.

I moved into the parish in June 1972 and was balancing the never-ending tension of parish involvement and the demands of a Master's program: classes, office calls, visits to the sick, some time for private prayer. Most days I hardly had time to look at a newspaper, but I thought I was doing pretty well, until October 23, 1972.

It had been one of those busy days to which I was becoming accustomed. When I returned to the rectory around three in the afternoon, I picked up the newspaper and went straight to the death notices. Perhaps it is just a peculiar quirk of my personality, but I usually start the paper — even today — by reading the obituaries. As I scanned the columns, my eye caught a name I recognized. It was a young man I had had as a client during my year in the drug-dependent unit. Dr. Elisabeth Kübler-Ross has written that one response to death is denial — people will not believe that this has happened. That was my first reaction. There must have been some mistake — or a coincidence perhaps. I even telephoned the funeral director. He assured me that "indeed it was Jimmy, the cause of death still 'under investigation,' and wasn't it a terrible tragedy. Thank you for calling, Father."

I thought back to the time I first met Jimmy. He was twenty, just a kid, likable enough, but with a persistent addiction to amphetamines and heroin, later to become an addiction to anything that could produce the strongest high in the shortest period of time. We developed a quick and strong bond, this crazy kid and I. I learned much about him in the weeks that we met together and we became very close. He was one of two children; his mother was the widow of a police officer who had died at an early age when their children, Jimmy and his sister, were babies. Thanks to the help of her own good parents she was able to work and provide a good home and plenty of love for her children. She was totally perplexed by her son's bizarre behavior when he was under the influence of whatever he could get his hands on. Placing him in this detoxification center was her final admission of defeat. She had done all she could and she had to look elsewhere for some kind of help. She never understood why he became chemically addicted. I was then and am still firmly convinced that Mary loved her son.

After my year at the hospital was completed and Jimmy was discharged, I only saw and heard from him sporadically. He said he wanted to stay in touch with me and I welcomed his contact, but it was so infrequent I often wondered how he was doing. Perhaps the twists and turns his life took after his release from the hospital and his consistent failures made him too ashamed to stay in touch. After his death I learned of his continuing trouble with the law, persistent drug abuse, and brief, unstable marriage. I had often considered taking the initiative — telephoning him periodically to see how things were going. And yet, everything I had learned in counseling told me that this was inappropriate. Even my supervisor discouraged it. And now he was dead.

Dead. What a final, thundering word. Dead. Beyond counseling — appropriate or inappropriate — beyond any kind of earthly help or human intervention, beyond everything. Dead.

I went that afternoon to the church to spend some time before the Blessed Sacrament. But prayer was no easy proposition. My anger kept getting in the way. Anger at myself; anger at Jimmy — even anger at God. I suppose that everyone who is involved in the so-called helping professions experiences this kind of anger at one time or another. We come to our jobs so often believing that there is nothing we can't accomplish. And all too often we are reminded of the limitations of our own fragile humanity. I had just been reminded of mine. I could not help Jimmy — no matter how I tried. And most frustrating of all was the slow realization that he had, perhaps, been beyond all help for some time; that he was, in a sense, doomed from the beginning; that it *had* to end this way.

I went to the wake and met Jimmy's family for the first time. As soon as I walked in the door of the funeral home his mother came toward me and said, "You don't need to tell me who you are. You're Father Copp. Jimmy used to talk about you all the time. I'd know you anywhere." She told me that he had been killed by a drug overdose — accidentally. He had lain in a coma for almost a week in the hospital before it proved to be too much for him and he died.

As I tried to say some prayers beside his lifeless body frustration rose again. He used to talk *about* me — why couldn't he have picked up a telephone and talked *to* me instead? There it was — the old familiar voice inside me saying "You can do *anything*. There isn't anyone who is beyond your help, if only you have the chance to give it." *if* I had been there; *if* I could have seen him regularly over the period of months since his discharge from the hospital; *if* I had been there, things would have been different. He used to talk about me — a fat lot of good that was doing everyone now!

Jimmy's mother asked me to deliver the homily at the Mass of Christian Burial the next day in their parish church. As I drove away from the wake I thought about the Scripture readings for the Funeral Mass that would

139

be the base for my talk. And it dawned on me that I was asking questions that had been asked countless times before. Martha accused Jesus at the death of her brother Lazarus — "Lord, if you had been here, my brother would never have died." And yet, He *wasn't* there. *Jesus wasn't there* to save Lazarus, his friend, from dying. Martha must have been angry — even more angry than I was at the moment. And yet, in a strange way, Jesus *had* been there. And He did something even more wonderful than keeping Lazarus from death. He allowed Lazarus to die so that he could be raised to life again. That was what it was all about. "I am the Resurrection and the Life. The man who believes in me, even if he should die, will come to life. And whoever is alive and believes in me will never die!"

I spoke at Jimmy's funeral the next day. That homily was, perhaps, the most difficult one I have ever preached. I addressed the anger, the questioning, the puzzling reality of Jimmy's death at the age of twenty-two with so much to live for and so much to share with those around him. As I looked out over the congregation that October morning, I was struck by the diversity of the crowd — family, friends, even some of the nursing staff from Massachusetts General Hospital where Jimmy had died — diversity and yet unity. We were mourning a son, a brother, a patient, a friend. I talked to myself a great deal before that Mass — talked myself into delivering a calm, hopeful, peace-filled proclamation of our faith in the resurrection ". . . the man who is alive and believes in me will never die." I quoted in my reflections the words of Kahlil Gibran the poet-philosopher who tells us that "remembrance is a form of meeting," and reminded the congregation that Jimmy lived on in us through our relationships with him and each other and most certainly lived on in the person of Christ who called him to life in Baptism, strengthened him through faith, and ultimately called him home to share eternal life. I'm sure that I believed those words that morning; I have come to understand them better as the years have gone on.

It has been almost eight years since that day in 1972. I still keep a picture of Jimmy on my study wall and think of him every once in a while. I suppose that I will never stop praying for him — remembering his anniversary and offering Mass for the repose of his soul. I suppose too, that one could consider a life so tragically shortened by such needless circumstances as having been wasted. But Jimmy's life was not wasted. He has taught those who knew him, certainly he taught me, a valuable lesson. Time and time again in my ministry, I have confronted the mystery of sudden and even violent deaths of young people. And time and time again I have had to grope for the right words to say to a stricken father, mother, or friend. I never approach these difficult tasks without thinking of Jimmy. It was through Jimmy that I first experienced the frustration of trying to help, but not being able to do enough; through him that I began to understand the bereaved parent, began to struggle with the eternal realities of death and life, to look for answers to the unanswerable questions, to try to make sense out of senseless tragedy. As I've searched and struggled I've drawn comfort from the text of the Mass of Christian Burial. "For those who have been faithful, life is changed, not ended. When the body of our earthly dwelling lies in death, we gain an everlasting dwelling place in heaven."

Rodney J. Copp

Dr. William M. Lamers, Jr., a founder and director of Hospice of Marin, shares his feelings about the death of his patients.

"I have a lot to learn from them ... Grief is the price I pay for love ... Each new loss makes me realize more clearly that I, too, will die."

The psychiatrist does not avoid being close to his patients, or crying with them. He reads poetry to comfort both them and himself.

When a person dies, Dr. Lamers attends the funeral to share in a public ceremony that has great social and psychological value.

HOW DOCTORS FEEL
WHEN A PATIENT DIES

Grief Is the Price for Love

I entered medical school in 1953 partly, I suppose, because I wanted to fight disease and have an element of control over death. Over the next five years of medical school and internship, I learned that there was no escape from death, no control over the powerful forces of grief and bereavement. I began training in psychiatry in 1958 and child psychiatry in 1961. By the time I went on active duty as a Navy physician in 1963, I was aware of work that had been done to understand why death affects us all so profoundly: Eric Lindemann's work on grief management in the aftermath of the Coconut Grove fire; Herman Feife's *The Meaning of Death*; Robert Fulton's *Death and Identity*. I began corresponding with the English psychiatrist John Bowlby and suddenly I felt as though someone had turned on a light in the dark room of grief. Bowlby began by studying juvenile delinquency and ended up looking at why children react so strongly to separation from their parents. His was the first study that began to explain why all of us react as strongly as we do to separation, loss, and death. He said that we all pass through a sequence of reactions to loss: *protest* ("Don't do this to me."), *despair* ("How can I possibly go on?"), and *detachment* ("No one would want me.").

In 1965 I developed a circular diagram to help explain the sequence of grief. To Bowlby's stages I added the dimensions of feelings (on the inside of the circle) and social and physical behavior (on the outside of the circle).

It has been helpful to me to know that progress through these stages and recovery from a death cannot be forced, that time is the crucial element. There are no "magic" things to say or do that will shorten or soften the often painful process of resolving grief.

During the early 1970s several friends of mine learned that they had incurable cancer and asked me to help arrange for them to die at home rather than in the hospital. I became aware that we were not doing a very good job of caring for dying persons or providing effective support for their families before and after the death. In 1974 I helped establish the second hospice program in the United States. Through hospice work I have learned that a great deal can be done to help patients who are dying; pain control and relief of symptoms have been greatly improved. With the assistance of a trained hospice team family members can do a good deal of the caregiving themselves in their own homes. Being able to "do something" is helpful to me as a physician; it's immeasurably helpful to a wife, husband, parent, or child when a member of the family is dying.

On a more personal level, I find it helpful to have experienced a great number of losses. It's not that I have become hardened to death or that this work is depressing; it's quite the contrary. But now I am relaxed about the

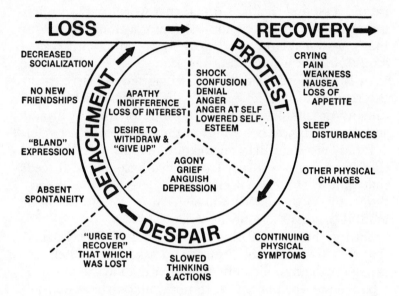

LOSS → RECOVERY →

DECREASED
SOCIALIZATION

PROTEST

DETACHMENT

DESPAIR

NO NEW
FRIENDSHIPS

"BLAND"
EXPRESSION

ABSENT
SPONTANEITY

APATHY
INDIFFERENCE
LOSS OF INTEREST

DESIRE TO
WITHDRAW &
"GIVE UP"

SHOCK
CONFUSION
DENIAL
ANGER
ANGER AT SELF
LOWERED SELF-
ESTEEM

AGONY
GRIEF
ANGUISH
DEPRESSION

CRYING
PAIN
WEAKNESS
NAUSEA
LOSS OF
APPETITE

SLEEP
DISTURBANCES

OTHER PHYSICAL
CHANGES

"URGE TO
RECOVER"
THAT WHICH
WAS LOST

SLOWED
THINKING
& ACTIONS

CONTINUING
PHYSICAL
SYMPTOMS

© 1978 William M. Lamers, Jr., M.D.

fact that I cry; I do not try to avoid becoming close to patients that I know will die. I have a lot to learn from them.

I am also comforted to learn that I am just like everyone else in my thoughts, feelings, and fears about death. Grief is the price I pay for love. Each new loss makes me realize more clearly that I, too, will die. Grief lessens my unreasonable hope for immortality and forces me to look at what I am doing with my time. I have the option of guarding my feelings and remaining uninvolved ... or I can continue to risk being involved knowing that there is no guarantee against losing again. My life and love are

144

tempered to a large degree by the experiences I have had through the deaths of friends. I am now beginning to see new meaning in the old saying "For it is only in daring to accept death that we may be said to truly possess life."

I have sometimes looked for ways to avoid grief, to minimize the pain of loss. After the death of a physician friend, I was surprised to find myself going home to bed in the middle of the day. But I was awakened within a few minutes by a powerful symbolic dream about the destruction of my medical school library. Grief work is difficult, pervasive, and takes time. There are no good shortcuts.

One day I visited a lady who was sad thinking of leaving her husband behind when she died. They had been exceptionally close and devoted over many good years of marriage. I asked if there was anything that I might do to ease her discomfort. She asked if I would read some of her favorite poems at my next visit. When I returned she produced a looseleaf book in which she had transcribed her favorite poems. As I leafed through the book, my eyes filled with tears because we shared many of the same favorite poems. Most of them dealt with a theme of loss. All were positive and supportive. I now have my own book of transcribed poems. I find myself going back to it for comfort and support.

POEMS I HAVE FOUND USEFUL

BRYANT, WILLIAM CULLEN "Thanatopsis"
DICKINSON, EMILY "The Dying Need But Little Dear"
GRAY, THOMAS "Elegy Written in a Country Churchyard"
HOPKINS, GERARD M. "Spring and Fall: To a Young Child"
HOUSMAN, A. E. "To an Athlete Dying Young"
LINDBERGH, ANNE MORROW "Revisitation"

Religion gives me a great deal of support. Belief in an afterlife and the potential for eventual reunion is comforting. Prayer and ceremony not only help to close a relationship that has ended with death, but provide a sense of satisfaction from knowing that important traditions have been fulfilled. All the talk of death in recent years has taken away some of the mystery about the scientific aspects of death ... and opened up for wonder the larger questions of life and death, time and eternity. Our search for knowledge has brought us back to fundamental questions that cannot be resolved by science and medicine. Religion offers a promise, a comfort, and a hope.

It is normal to want to withdraw and avoid people after a death. Oftentimes I don't know what to say. A warm hug can take the place of words. I know how difficult it is to live with regrets for not having done something or said something to try to ease another's grief. I find it helpful to *do* something when I am grieving or when I want to support a grieving person. It is usually best to keep it simple; a few words, a phone call, a note, or a visit. Nothing I can say can take away another's grief, but the comfort that comes from a friend can sustain me.

In hospice work I have found it helpful to attend funeral services for the patients who have died. This gives me a chance to *do* something: to show my support for the family, to show my respect for the person who died. By uniting in celebrating the life that was lived, I can share in public ceremony that has great social and psychological value. At a time when the natural tendency is to withdraw, the funeral brings people together. When the natural tendency is toward inaction, the funeral encourages activity and participation. When strong feelings tend to block the normal flow of speech, the funeral encourages expression, ritual, singing, and the exchange of greetings and support. For me, participation in the funeral is a bridge leading to support in the months of bereavement that follow death.

I am pleased with the changes I have seen in the last quarter of a century. But I am also aware that we have a long way to go to reach a point where we again recognize the naturalness of death and begin to live more comfortably with it. I can only hope.

William M. Lamers, Jr.

AFTERWORD

BY EARL A. GROLLMAN

A first child was born to David and Bathsheba. The youngster became critically ill. The father exchanged his royal garments for simple sackcloth, refused to eat, and spent every available moment with his offspring. Shortly thereafter, the infant died.

David rose up from his place, put on his regal clothing, and began to eat a sumptuous meal. His followers were puzzled over the strange contrast between his behavior before and after his son's death.

David explained as follows: "While the child was yet alive, I fasted and wept; for I said, 'Who knoweth whether the Lord will not be gracious to me, that the child may live?' But now that he is dead, wherefore shall I fast? Can I bring him back again?"

Your loved one is dead. It may not be fair, but it is a fact that has to be accepted. You cannot bring that person back again to life.

You can, however, learn from the wise king. Courage is not the absence of fear and pain, but the affirmation of life despite fear and pain.

No matter how great your pain, there is hope and help for the future. As your sense of humor returns and you find yourself laughing, you're feeling better. As you begin to make major decisions about your life, you're getting better still. When you are able to take out the mementos of your beloved and smile through your tears at memories of happiness together, you're much improved. And when you learn that no one can bring back your loved one, that it's your job to pick up and go on living, then you'll know you are truly growing and recovering yourself.

Other Sources of Help

Grief shared is grief diminished. There are many sources of help from organizations of people who have suffered similar bereavements to individual professional grief counselors. You need not be alone during these difficult times.

Bereaved Parents Organizations

"The death of a child seems so wrong ... Children should not die before their parents do."

Children's deaths are especially difficult to comprehend and manage. Just as they are beginning to live, life is taken from them. As they start to be actively productive, their activity is stilled forever.

Parents are desperately in need of help when a child dies. Because of their anguish over their loss, their marriage may be in jeopardy. Surviving children may mistake their parents' anguish for an indication that they loved their dead child more than they love them.

Bereaved parents organizations reach out and share what they have mutually experienced. They help each other to accept the reality of their loss, to live more comfortably with their memories of the past, and to learn to reinvest themselves emotionally by reconstructing their lives.

The contributors, Carolyn Szybist of the National Sudden Infant Death Syndrome Foundation; Grace Powers Monaco of Candlelighters; and Paula Shamres of the Society of Compassionate Friends, are eloquent representatives of their excellent parent support groups.

National Sudden Infant Death Syndrome Foundation
301 S. Michigan Avenue
Chicago, Illinois 60604

Candlelighters
123 C Street, S.E.
Washington, D.C. 20003

The Society of Compassionate Friends
P.O. Box 1347
Oak Brook, Illinois 60521

American Gold Star Mothers, Inc.
2128 Leroy Place, N.W.
Washington, D.C. 20008

Clergy and Religious Agencies

It is natural to turn to the clergy during the crisis of death. As an expositor of the mysteries of God, the minister or priest or rabbi can render a measure of friendship, forgiveness, and spiritual understanding. Though each denomination has differing beliefs and practices, all religions are united in the goal of offering emotional and religious guidance "through the valley of the shadow of death."

You might contact the person who officiated at the funeral of your loved one for help. Or the following organizations and agencies could be of assistance:

NONDENOMINATIONAL:

The American Association of Pastoral Counselors
3 West 29th Street
New York, New York 10001

PROTESTANT:

National Council of the Churches of Christ
475 Riverside Drive
New York, New York 10027

CATHOLIC:

National Conference of Catholic Charities
1346 Connecticut Avenue
New York, New York 10027

JEWISH:

Council of Jewish Federations
315 Park Avenue South
New York, New York 10010

Guidance and Family Associations

For help during this difficult period you might consult your local mental health clinic, social service organization, or one of the following organizations:

Family Service Association of America
44 East 23rd Street
New York, New York 10010

National Association for Mental Health
1800 North Kent Street
Arlington, Virginia 22209

National Council on Family Relations
1219 University Avenue, S.E.
Minneapolis, Minnesota 55414

United Way of America
801 North Fairfax Street
Alexandria, Virginia 22314

Help for Your Children

Many boys without a father need a man with whom to identify. For information concerning the local organizations, contact:

Big Brothers of America
220 Suburban Station Building
Philadelphia, Pennsylvania 19103

A widower who feels that his daughter should have the companionship of a woman volunteer should call:

Big Sisters of America
220 Suburban Station Building
Philadelphia, Pennsylvania 19103

To find the local chapter of the international organization that has done so much to enhance the welfare of single parents and their children contact:

Parents Without Partners
7910 Woodmont Avenue
Washington, D.C. 20014

Psychological, Psychiatric, and Social Work Counselors

The major associations with accredited professionals and services are:

PSYCHOLOGICAL:

American Psychological Association
1200 17th Street, N.W.
Washington, D.C. 20036

PSYCHIATRIC:

American Psychiatric Association
1700 18th Street
Washington, D.C. 20009

American Psychoanalytic Association
1 East 57th Street
New York, New York 10022

SOCIAL WORK:

National Association of Social Workers
1425 H Street, N.W.
Washington, D.C. 20005

Widow-Widower Groups

You are used to a *we* relationship. What shall *we* give our children for their birthdays? How shall *we* keep up with inflation? Where shall *we* live during our retirement years? A life of sharing is a way of life that is so agonizing to sever. It is difficult to change *we* to *me*. Even the words *widow* and *widower* are difficult to say. Nevertheless, the altered status must be confronted.

Widow-widower groups exist in virtually every city and town in our country. Most programs are based on the premise that a bereaved person is best able to reach out to other bereft people in aiding their adjustment to their new lives. In these groups, the emphasis is upon counseling, group discussions, community education, and pleasant sociability.

THEOS is a well-known international group for widows, which was founded by Bea Decker, the mother of Roberta Decker, a contributor to this book:

They Help One Another Spiritually (THEOS)
Office Building Penn Hills Mall
Suite 306
Pittsburgh, Pennsylvania 15235

For further information about the organizations in your community contact your clergyperson, funeral director, social service agency or:

Laboratory of Community Psychiatry
Harvard Medical School
58 Fernwood Road
Boston, Massachusetts 02115

Widowed Personal Services
National Association of Retired People (NARP)
1909 K Street, N.W.
Washington, D.C. 20049